A BEGINNER'S GUIDE
TO CREATING REALITY

THIRD EDITION

RAMTHA

A BEGINNER'S GUIDE TO CREATING REALITY

THIRD EDITION

An Introduction to Ramtha and His Teachings

JZK Publishing
A Division of JZK, Inc.

**A BEGINNER'S GUIDE
TO CREATING REALITY**
THIRD EDITION

FOURTH PRINTING ❦ JUNE 2008

ISBN # 1-57873-027-9

JZK Publishing
Ramtha's School of Enlightenment
A Division of JZK, Inc.

P.O. Box 1210
Yelm, Washington 98597
360.458.5201
800.347.0439
www.ramtha.com
www.jzkpublishing.com

"Behold, there came unto me a sweet maiden as you have not seen, whose gilded hairs danced about her. The crown that be upon her hair was not of lilies or rosebuds or irises but an unknown flower. Her drapery, indeed her gowns, were translucent, mellow, and free. She came unto me and gave me a great sword. It sang. It sang. Yet it took nine hands to hold its handle, it was so great."

"It was the Isness that formulated itself into an apparition of the most beautiful sort. She gave me the sword and said, 'Here, Ram, go and conquer yourself.' "

— *Ramtha*

CONTENTS

PART I
RAMTHA, A MASTER'S JOURNEY TO ENLIGHTENMENT

PART II
FUNDAMENTAL CONCEPTS OF RAMTHA'S TEACHINGS

FIGURES

ACKNOWLEDGMENTS

Our sincere thanks and appreciation to everyone who jointly helped bring about this book. It was an arduous teamwork effort inspired by the same love we all share for our Master Teacher, Ramtha, and his words of wisdom.

We would like to acknowledge Debbie Christie for making the original recordings of Ramtha's words available for transcription. We appreciate the copyediting work of Pat Richker and her zealous dedication in keeping the words of the Master pure. Many thanks to Stephanie Millham for her careful proofreading and professionalism. Special thanks to Jaime Leal-Anaya for the literary edition of this book, the construction of Ramtha's Glossary, the Index, and the introductory essay to Ramtha's teachings.

Finally, we would like to extend our gratitude to JZ Knight for her dedication to the Great Work and for making Ramtha's teachings available to everyone who wants to hear them and venture into the exploration of the great unknown.

FOREWORD BY JZ KNIGHT

"Know yourself and you will know the universe and the Gods."
Inscription in the Temple of Delphi

Dear Reader:

The following book is based on the concept of an ancient mystery school brought into the close of the twentieth century, an age which wallows in alarming materialism where neither the church, imprisoned by its own dogma and political intrigues, nor science, locked within the confines of matter, knows how to make individuals whole. Science need not change its methods, only broaden its scope; and religion need not change its traditions but rather remember its origins: the Spirit and its primal significance. The restoration of the link between the visible and the invisible for the useful application of the omnipotent in our everyday lives becomes the new conscious bridge to traverse the abyss that separates heaven from earth. Such a labor is called the Great Work. The concept of Ramtha's School of Ancient Wisdom is one whose academy is being built as each initiate/student becomes the individual building stone.

At the heart of the mystery school is what Ramtha refers to as the Void: one vast nothing materially, yet all things potentially, and Pythagoras referred to as the Absolute. This is the essence of the uncreated being, the uncreated God, the nothing from which all potentials spring. The Void is the great nonmanifest from which the ephemeral worlds are made manifest. As the manifest worlds change and eventually pass away, the Void remains unchanged. This eternal essence has been concealed from humanity, for man only perceives the things of tangible form, not knowing that these forms are combined with the infinite. Is it then possible for humanity to know what is concealed from them or, as Pythagoras asked, has anyone ever seen the master of time, the soul of the suns, the source of intelligence?

Ramtha teaches that one cannot see the Void or see the unchangeable, for to do so would declare a separateness from that which we ineffably are. We can only become one with it and in this way define a relationship that results in the bestowing of dimension, intelligence, and essence to things of form. It is precisely this divine relationship that God as moving Spirit is thus defined. We, humanity, are the Gods that bring the harmony that exists between what is seen and not seen. When becoming or being the Void, the student can begin to fathom this center of all things and in this the Great Work begins. The student undergoes initiations that bring closer the divine relationship by resembling the Gods that work the fires of creation. The work of the school is the combining of the scientific knowledge with the esoteric understanding of Spirit, coupled with the mastery of things through will, thus mastering the personal storms that divide the individual against the unity that manifests God as self.

Ramtha refers to us as the forgotten Gods, an appropriate statement considering what most consider God to be — a magnificence that created humanity but remains apart and distant from them — thus forgetting our own divine origins and activities, which have themselves defined the term God. Gods did not preexist all else but rather the Void was first, eternal, and absolute. The Void through an unimaginable contemplation created a principal point, which Ramtha refers to as Point Zero. This point contained consciousness and energy potentially and was the child of the Void. Point Zero was an indivisible substance, which contained infinite consciousness and energy, the primal fire that would form the engines of creation. This is the Spirit, the essence of everything, and it is this essence which constitutes the definition of God as ourselves. We, the Spirit, are the first principle embodying divine faculties. The metaphor of the mystic lotus can help us understand this more clearly. Imagine for a moment an Egyptian initiate, lying in her sepulcher, who sees emerging from the blackness of a starless night a brilliant point of light. The point slowly begins to open like a radiating flower, with its incandescent center unfolding and spreading out like a rose of brilliant light with a thousand petals. We are the flower unfolding from the Source. From that moment God is manifest — we, you, I. From that moment, we too contemplated and doubled the self into divisible substance. We now possess the active ingredient of consciousness and energy, represented in the ancient schools of thought as the eternal masculine (consciousness) and the eternal feminine (energy). Thus this perfect union of consciousness and energy forms the perfect union of generative and reproductive faculty, which later would generate the world and the essence of God as indeed ourselves. It is this union that is responsible for the unfolding of God in time, dimension, and space.

God, as ourselves, can now be defined as the human being, a body garment worn by God as Spirit for the purpose of making known the unknown in the physicality of the three-dimensional world. The soul of man records this progress in holographic energy forms as a log of the journey. This blending of body as garment, soul as memory, and Spirit as God working in distinct harmony is what facilitates the creation of reality. The knowledge of these is the actual key to life from the constitution of the cell to the hyperphysical constitution of humanity as God. The triad of the threefold nature of body, soul, and Spirit produces the phenomena we refer to as the mind of man, which constructs thought-forms around which energy is patterned, creating the fluid of cosmic reality. Humanity alone is responsible for evolving matter held in earthly roots for the purpose of experiencing these in physicality and bringing forth all potentials from the Void into a knowable experience. These creative thoughts bring worlds into evolution, removing veil after veil from the process of divinity itself.

— JZ Knight

INTRODUCTORY ESSAY
TO RAMTHA'S TEACHINGS

A Unique Metaphysical System of Thought

The teachings of Ramtha are a unique metaphysical system of thought. It requires a very careful examination and consideration in order to grasp the full meaning and impact of its content. We say that Ramtha's teachings are metaphysical in nature because they address the fundamental questions about human existence and the human person, about our destiny and origins, about the nature of good and evil, the soul, death and life, the world, and our relationship to others.

Ramtha's system of thought is unique, well-structured, and comprehensive both in its content and in the format in which it is conveyed. It provides a world-view, an approach to reality that places in context and removes the mystery from many questions that have enraptured great philosophers and thinkers through the ages.

> "So what are the teachings of the Great Work that you have come to listen to? They are not about the occult work and indeed they are not about New Age. The message I give you is the foundations of the Earth, the cosmos. That is not new at all. The message I am telling you is this: that if you be God — and indeed you are, philosophically speaking, that is — that should be an enticement to experience that nearer to that principle."[1]

1 *Ramtha's Introduction to the World Tour*, video ed. (Yelm: JZK Publishing, a division of JZK, Inc., 1998).

The format in which Ramtha's teachings are conveyed is intrinsic to the message itself. The teachings are not simply an intellectual dissertation on specific subjects or a mere intellectual analysis of them, nor are they a form of revealed truth that requires the blind allegiance of faith. Ramtha's teachings are not a new religion nor are they the building blocks of a new church. His teachings are a system of thought that contains within its approach to reality the elements and mechanisms that allow the individual to engage Ramtha's philosophy and verify and experience its content firsthand. In other words, this unique aspect of the teachings allows the philosophy, or the *concepts of reality,* to be experienced and become instead *wisdom about the nature of reality.*

Enlightenment:
Turning the Philosophy into Wisdom

This particular quality of Ramtha's system of thought resembles the initiations into sacred knowledge practiced by the ancient mystery schools of Greece, Egypt, and the Middle East as well as the ancient gnostic schools of the Middle East and Europe. It is important to note that this characteristic distinguishes Ramtha's teachings from the traditional philosophical schools of the western world.

The main differences we find are in the concepts of truth and in the understanding of the person's ability to acquire new knowledge. A person's knowledge is not only empirical or scientific in nature, according to Ramtha, but it can also become the person's own truth and personal experience. Ramtha distinguishes between these two approaches to the learning process and describes them in terms of binary mind and analogical mind. Binary mind refers to the empirical and scientific modes of knowledge that rely on intellectual analysis and observation through the senses. Analogical mind is when the individual learns new knowledge by becoming analogous with the subject of learning, by becoming and experiencing the very subject of observation as well as being the Observer aware of the experience itself. For Ramtha, a piece of information that remains impersonal to the individual is not real knowledge but simply theory or philosophy and potential wisdom. Information and theories that have been experienced analogically as the Observer and the action itself are, on the other hand, real knowledge, wisdom, and truth.

> "I am here to teach you truth. Truth will be what you experience. Everything I tell you is merely philosophy. But if my philosophy, as it were, can only be argued by doubt, then the only way that we conquer doubt is to emerge in truth. And the only way we get that, my beloved people, is to experience the philosophy, for if you experience it and it manifests, then it is no longer philosophy; it is your truth."[2]

In this sense Ramtha follows more closely the ancient Middle-Eastern understanding of the concept of truth rather than the Greek and modern one. The Hebrew word for truth — אמת, "a'meth" — contains three letters: aleph, mêm, and taw, the first, middle, and last letters of the Hebrew alphabet. This arrangement of the Hebrew word for truth expresses a sense of completeness and wholeness. This word was used to express something that had been experienced and known, an action of the past, and never referring simply to an isolated piece of information or data. The Greek translation of the Hebrew word for truth — αληθεια, "aletheia" — lost the experiential character of the concept

---

2 *Ramtha's Introduction to the World Tour,* video ed.

and referred to it in terms of mere information found or accepted as true by a consensus. A person's ability to acquire knowledge became limited to the scientific method, which is based on observation and analysis aided by the intellect and the senses alone.

What we find in the traditional western understanding of objective knowledge and truth is a fundamental assumption about the human person and the nature of reality. The scientific method limits its range of attainable knowledge to phenomena that can be observed and verified through the senses of the physical body. Anything outside this range is consigned to the realm of myth and folklore. In other words, the nature of reality and the human person are nothing more than their physical nature and materiality. Sigmund Freud's psychoanalysis and profile of the human psyche are a clear example of this trend.

The physical body and the material world, in Ramtha's thought, are only one aspect of the real world. In fact, they are only the product and effect of the real world constituted by consciousness and energy. The human person is best described as consciousness and energy creating the nature of reality. The physical world is only one of seven levels of expression of consciousness and energy. Ramtha uses the concept of the Observer from quantum theory to explain his concept of consciousness and energy. He also uses the concept of God as creator and sovereign to describe the human person as consciousness and energy.

> "The greatest teaching that was ever given is that you are God, truly. And life is that which is termed the gift of God, a divine presence, of making known the unknown, of that which is termed an opportunity coming from a light review to clean up our business, our unfinished handiwork of past lives."

"We came back here not to build great cathedrals to God but do that small business of cleaning up our confusion of who and what we really are. If we are — and I can tell you this — Gods, let me also add that what I tell you is not the truth, for truth is subjective reality that is a prize that belongs to all of us potentially."[3]

The concept of enlightenment then, in the light of these considerations from Ramtha's system of thought, is when people experience the philosophy and realize fully and consciously that they are a divine being, that they are God, the creator of their own reality and destiny, that they are consciousness and energy creating the nature of reality, the Observer of quantum mechanics. This is the context in which Ramtha describes himself as Ramtha the Enlightened One.

A person who is seeking knowledge, in order to become enlightened, is a person seeking new models of thought unknown to them, which they can experience and thus gain wisdom. The basic driving force moving consciousness and energy to evolve and expand itself, to know itself beyond the already known, is the intent to make known the unknown. The seven levels of creation are the result of consciousness and energy evolving and expanding its reflection of itself into the unknown. Since in Ramtha's view of reality the human person is not the physical body but consciousness and energy manifesting through a physical body, the attainment of knowledge and wisdom is not limited by space, time, and the laws of physics. The only limitation on the person knowing and experiencing something lies in the ability to think and imagine it intellectually so that it may serve as a paradigm for a new experience and potential wisdom.

---

3 *Ramtha's Introduction to the World Tour,* video ed.

"I am a teacher that teaches to that which is termed my people the potentials that they have not dreamt, nor thought, nor dreamed and conceived that they could possibly be. I teach them that they are. And the moment that I teach them that they are, they captivate the thought in the neuronet of their brain and they ponder it. And if they ponder it dutifully and accept — if they can say to me, 'I accept; it feels so right to me; I accept' — if they accept that, they never have to be afraid or worry, because they are on automatic because the will of God has accepted the dream. And that dream takes them to a new paradigm of experience, a new life, a life that is much more than hope. It is everything they never could have dreamed about. There is where I am the teacher."[4]

Ramtha's Specific Teaching Format

It is easy for many sectors of society today to dismiss Ramtha's teachings straightaway due to the highly unusual way in which they are conveyed. Unfortunately, it is an all-too-common response to attach a judgment to a message based on the form in which it is presented rather than on the content of what is presented. Marketing, communications, and the techniques of publicity, selling, and advertising are sublime examples of this.

The uncommon form in which Ramtha delivers his teachings is by no means arbitrary and superficial. He has pointed out explicitly the reasons behind such a format and explained that in order to grasp his message, it is important to become aware of the paradigms of thought, the roots of preconceived ideas, unconscious prejudices, and molds in which we normally perceive and evaluate reality.

4 *JZ Knight and Ramtha: Intimate Conversations*, video ed. (Yelm: JZK Publishing, a division of JZK, Inc., 1998).

Right from the moment our parents teach us their language in childhood, we are subjected to a number of preconceived ideas about God, the nature of reality, physics, and psychology: God is an entity of male gender who lives in a place called heaven; all strangers are dangerous; the dark is a fearful place; certain diseases cannot be cured; the winner takes it all, and the strong and the beautiful rule. These preconceived ideas may never be consciously addressed and evaluated by the individual, yet they form part of the way in which their reality is perceived and experienced every day.

Ramtha's teaching techniques often seek to challenge the individual as well as offer them the tools to become aware of those preconceived ideas that shape and set the boundaries in which we normally perceive reality. The purpose of this is to allow as a result the emergence of a broader perspective of mind which would enable us to experience reality in a more meaningful, unlimited, conscious, and extraordinary way as well as to provide us with a greater spectrum of potentiality for our experience than was previously available to us.

> "I am here to teach you how to no longer live in denial, how to understand to be nearer to God, how to access that in you. And it is all philosophy, but it brings with it a practical experience to put to challenge the senses and put to challenge the body. And if God lives within you, then God shall rise up and will accomplish these marvels to which the senses and the body simply and utterly fail to do. And then we have a wildly, beauteous testament. And then we have joy to the greatest magnitude, that what lives in us is a hope beyond hope, that there is more to us than the reflection in the mirror, and there is much more to us than what religion and politics and boundaries and

the color of skin and sexuality have had to offer in these most tedious and trying of times."[5]

Channeling Ramtha — What Is Important Is the Message

One of the more controversial aspects of Ramtha's teachings is the form in which he chose to deliver his message. Ramtha in presenting his philosophy as the fruit of his own truth and personal experience makes the point that he himself is the embodiment of the philosophy, the living representation and manifestation of his thought. Thus he says that he is an immortal God, consciousness and energy, and that he lived once as a human being 35,000 years ago in the long-gone continent of Lemuria. He explains that in that lifetime he addressed the questions about human existence and the meaning of life, and that through his own observation, reflection, and contemplation he became enlightened and conquered the physical world and death. He has taught that he realized a way in which to take his body with him to a level of mind in which his true essence as consciousness and energy could remain fully conscious, be completely free and unlimited to experience any and all aspects of creation, and continue to make known the unknown. He refers to this process as his ascension.

The fact that he is no longer limited by his physical body allows his consciousness and energy to interact with the physical world in other forms. He often refers to himself as being the wind pushing the clouds, for example, or as being the morning, or a stranger, or a beggar on the street observing civilizations come and go, or as anything that consciousness would dare to imagine.

5 *Ramtha's Introduction to the World Tour,* video ed.

The form in which he communicates his teachings is through the phenomenon called channeling. In fact, it was Ramtha who made the term known. He uses the body of JZ Knight to channel himself and teach his philosophy in person. JZ Knight is the only channel he has chosen and uses to deliver his message. During her initial encounters with Ramtha in 1977, she explains:

"And when Ramtha started teaching me how to leave my body, this was very interesting because it was like dying. And he said, 'This is what you are going to experience the moment of death.' Well, now what would you do? If he comes up to you and he says, 'You are going to die, but it won't hurt, and it will only be a little short while and then you are going to come back,' would you trust this guy? It is like an anesthesiologist: Now go to sleep and be nice, you know. Ramtha said, 'This is what you have to do,' and he gave me some words I had to say and a focus point. And he worked with me and he said, 'This is how I used to leave my body. This is how I developed this companionship with the wind.'

"And so I get to a point and I would focus on this artificial vase of plastic daisies in front of me that were sitting on the coffee table. And I am sitting on this chair, and I would get to this point and nothing would happen. He said, 'You don't have to hold your breath to die. Why do you have to hold your breath? You don't have to hold your breath. You don't have to grip the chair. Just relax.'

"So I did it again. And then all of a sudden I was chasing that light at the end of the tunnel and this wind was whizzing by me. And the moment I hit that light that was so bright, I was up against a light wall. And I remember I never saw Ramtha but I remember him talking to me. And he was talking, and it was really beautiful and loving. He said, 'Now you are your true self at this moment. This moment is who you really are, and you have left your body behind.'

"And I noticed that in that moment I had no pain. I had no concept of weight. I had no concept of dimension because I had no body in order to define dimension. And I noticed that at that point I had no fear. I felt like this was the most natural place. Like a fish in the ocean, I felt like that this was my natural ocean.

"And then he brought me back and I noticed my body; my heart was beating very, very fast. And I noticed it took awhile for my body to just calm down — and it did — because while I was gone, Ramtha put his energy into the body. He wore it for forty-five minutes. And when he left it, I put it back on."[6]

The Value of Women — A Holistic Approach

Ramtha's choice to channel his message through a woman, rather than by using his own physical body, is making the statement that God and the divine are not the prerogative of men alone and that women are worthy expressions of the divine, capable of genius and of being God realized. It is also asserting that what is important in his philosophy is not the worshiping of the messenger or a face or an image — which caused the collapse of so many efforts to enlighten in the past — but to listen to the message itself. It is also making the statement that the true essence of the human person is not limited to the physical body or a specific gender. The phenomenon of channeling is made possible therefore within the framework of Ramtha's system of thought. In other words, channeling as it happens in the person of JZ Knight is possible only if Ramtha's teachings are true.

---

6 JZ Knight's introductory talk in *Beginning C&E® Workshop*, October 7-8, 1995, Tape 324 ed. (Yelm: Ramtha Dialogues, 1995).

"And Ramtha said, 'Well, I am going to, with your permission, use your body for a period of time.'

"And I said, 'Yes. What are you going to do with it?'

"And he said, 'Well, I am going to use it to teach.'

"I thought, well, why would you want to use my body? You are beautiful. Why don't you just come on out and show it how it is.'

"And he said, 'It doesn't work that way,' he said, 'because people in this civilization are image prone and they are idol prone. They have been immersed in the Catholic religion. They have been immersed in the Christian tradition. They believe God lives outside of them instead of inside of them. They believe that God is a man. They believe that Christ was a man. They believe in images but not in themselves. So,' he said, 'I remain imageless.' He said, 'But I am going to teach through your body, and everyone knows it is not my body.'

"And I said, 'Yes, but I am a woman. I am a girl. I have, you know, things.'

"And he said, 'I know.' He said, 'Women are the most prejudiced group of people that ever lived because women have never been afforded the divine right of God, and they have no ally in heaven.' That is what he said. And he said, 'So women have been abused by men and herded by men through religion to perform according to those religious doctrines. And in fact women were despised by Jehovah. So,' he said, 'it is important that when the teachings come through, they come through the body of a woman so that women, when they hear, realize that God isn't a father but God is also a mother, and that God is both father and mother and neither, and that the Christ is not a man but has been many men and now will be many women, and that to be a son of God is also to be a daughter of God.'

"And he said, 'The greatest quest is for women to take the equality of their divinity and utilize it without any encumbrances from any men.' And he said, 'To tell a woman to go and look in the mirror and say now you are looking in the face of God is a challenge because they don't believe you. If you tell a woman go and look in the face of God, and you send them to a chapel and you have them look in the face of a suffering Jesus hanging on the cross, they will believe you. But they don't believe in themselves.' I understood that."[7]

Scientific Scrutiny of Channeling

The veracity of this phenomenon points to the truth of Ramtha's message. This is an important point to consider because the advance of science has developed tests and equipment that can scrutinize this phenomenon and study it from a physiological, neurological, and psychological point of view. Scientific techniques now exist to study the phenomenon of channeling by JZ Knight and to rule out the possibility of fraud. These scientific studies took place in 1996 when a distinguished panel of eighteen scholars — comprised of scientists, psychologists, sociologists, and religious experts — studied JZ Knight before, during, and after channeling Ramtha.

A team of highly qualified psychologists — headed by Dr. Stanley Krippner, Ph.D., of Saybrook Institute Graduate School — studied JZ Knight and her school for a year and then conducted a number of psychological and physiological tests with the latest technology and equipment available. They concluded that the readings taken from JZ Knight's autonomic nervous system responses were so dramatic that they categorically ruled out any possibility of conscious fakery, schizophrenia, or multiple-personality disorders.

---

7 JZ Knight's introductory talk in *Beginning C&E® Workshop*, October 7-8, 1995, Tape 324 ed. (Yelm: Ramtha Dialogues, 1995).

Dr. Stanley Krippner described himself as "extremely skeptical and yet open-minded" before performing the tests in collaboration with world-renowned neuroscientist Ian Wickramasekera, Ph.D., a fellow professor at Saybrook Institute Graduate School. Dr. Krippner said, "When we were testing JZ, Ian was quite astonished because the needles on his polygraph that were graphing all of the psychophysiological responses literally jumped from one part of the page to the other part of the page when Ramtha entered the picture. And he had never seen such a dramatic change. . . . She's not faking it because when we hooked her up to test her physiological responses, we got results which could not have been manipulated."[8]

According to Wickramasekera, who is president-elect of the Association for Applied Psychophysiology and Biofeedback in Colorado, when JZ Knight went into trance and the consciousness of Ramtha took over her body, her heart rate hit a low of 40 beats per minute and then raced to 180 beats per minute. In her normal, resting state, Knight's heart rate was between 85 and 90. He pointed out that "You might see this in someone who is jogging or having a serious panic attack, but at the time JZ Knight was sitting completely still. . . . It became apparent to the research team that something very dramatic and physiological was going on, and something that on the basis of everything that is known about human capacities cannot be faked." Dr. Krippner explained that "An individual cannot really fake, cannot really role-play because in hypnosis there's barely any physiological change at all. In role-playing there's basically very little change at all."[9]

---

8 These quotes were taken from various interviews that took place during the conference *In Search of the Self: The Role of Consciousness in the Construction of Reality, a Conference on Contemporary Spirituality,* February 8-9, 1997, Yelm, Washington, video ed. (Yelm: JZK Publishing, a division of JZK, Inc., 1997).
9 Ibid.

Dr. Gail Harley pointed out that "Her eyes changed from a soft striking blue as JZ Knight to an unfocused deep steel gray as Ramtha. Her skin tone darkens and her jaw stiffens, as her bearing becomes more militant and formal as Ramtha. Her stride becomes stiffly gaited." Dr. Harley concluded Knight could not be playacting or performing as Ramtha. "The dramatic changes in her appearance when Ramtha is in control are far too stringent to suggest that." JZ Knight and some students who were tested rated extremely high in their hypnotic abilities, which was a significant finding because the relationship between hypnotic ability and bipolar personality and other organic disorders is counterbalancing: When one goes up, the other goes down. Dr. Krippner explained that "You cannot have both."[10]

After noticing all of this dramatic data being collected, Dr. Krippner said offhandedly to JZ as they were leaving the building, "Well, JZ, I don't know what you are, but at least you're not a fake and not a fraud." Dr. Krippner said, "Little did I know that that offhand statement just meant so much to her because of all the accusations thrown her way over the years. Ian and I were quite surprised that the data were as dramatic and unique as they were. Neither Ian nor I had any hesitation about getting the word out."[11] Wickramasekera presented this material to the American Psychological Association, which is a prestigious venue for such work. Dr. Krippner also presented the findings at a number of scientific conventions. The first article to be published on this work, "The Ramtha Phenomenon: Psychological, Phenomenological, and Geomagnetic Data,"

---

10 *In Search of the Self: The Role of Consciousness in the Construction of Reality,* video ed.
11 Ibid.

was published in *The Journal of the American Society for Psychical Research* in January of 1998.[12]

> "And don't be bothered and worried and be afraid. Don't be afraid of what I have told you. And don't dismiss me as my daughter or dismiss me as a fraud. My God, man, have more intelligence than that. Listen to the message. That is what is important here. And the message is saying nothing bad about you at all. It is saying everything wonderful about you."[13]

Ramtha the Teacher and Hierophant

The teachings of Ramtha have an explicit and an implicit aspect. His teachings are like the creation of an artist that contains both a specific message *from* the artist and a more general message that speaks *about* the artist. Since Ramtha teaches from personal experience and not from intellectual speculation, as we explained earlier, Ramtha *is* his teachings. To have an insight into the person of Ramtha is to have an insight into his teachings.

His in-depth knowledge of how the brain works and his personal understanding of human nature give him the ability to deliver his message in such a way that the student can more effectively grasp and understand it. He takes into account the varied cultural, philosophical, and religious backgrounds of his audience in his use of imagery, words, examples, definition of terms, and concepts that appeal and are familiar to each student. Ramtha is a dynamic teacher.

---

12 Stanley Krippner, Ian Wickramasekera, Judy Wickramasekera, and Charles W. Winstead, III, "The Ramtha Phenomenon: Psychological, Phenomenological, and Geomagnetic Data," in *The Journal of the American Society for Psychical Research*, No. 92, January 1998.

13 *JZ Knight and Ramtha: Intimate Conversations*, video ed.

He does not limit himself to a purely discursive presentation of his message but incorporates into it actions, music, disciplines, and vivid examples that engage the students, giving them a greater insight into what is being taught.

Sometimes he engages the audience in deep philosophical contemplation of a specific subject and at other times he uses dramatization to empower his message. For example, one of the ways in which he explains the concept of the Void contemplating itself, and consciousness and energy creating seven levels of reality is through a powerful and dramatic pagan dance.

Ramtha goes to great lengths to make his whole audience move at the same pace of understanding. He insists continuously on the importance of the students articulating and explaining to each other each segment of the teaching. This ensures that the whole audience is grasping the teaching and allows Ramtha to more powerfully address the specific background and level of understanding of the people listening to him.

Once the philosophical aspect of the teaching has been given, Ramtha initiates the student into that knowledge so that it may be turned into personal experience and wisdom. These initiations take the form of various disciplines of his design where the student has the opportunity to engage the knowledge. Ramtha differs from other teachers in this aspect. He takes on the role of a Master Teacher and Hierophant, a teacher who has the power to manifest what he speaks and intends. This is an important aspect of the teachings that likens it to the gnostic, philosophical movement and the ancient mystery schools. A close examination of Ramtha's system of thought shows a clear distinctiveness in form and content from what is traditionally known as Gnosticism and the philosophy of the mystery schools. Ramtha himself does not refer to his system of thought in these terms; rather he calls it the School of Ancient Wisdom, the wisdom of the ages.

> "For I am the Hierophant that will initiate you into God, and I am the one that will teach you to surrender to it. But it will be that which is termed your own God that will take you to these far-flung places and enable you to do the remarkable that the personality, for all of your intellectual glory, could never, ever accomplish even in ten million lifetimes."[14]

Given all these considerations, the reader must be aware that Ramtha's teachings in printed form capture only part of the teaching presentation since they miss the dynamic element of the teachings, the voice inflection, the teaching without words, and its application in action.

Ramtha's Use of Language

He has delineated a unique understanding of language. As in every philosophy, the importance of the language and terminology used to convey its concepts is vital to ensure further dialogue and analysis of such concepts and philosophies.

In Ramtha's system of thought, the problem of language becomes very acute. Firstly, the English language is not Ramtha's original form of communication. Secondly, the concepts he endeavors to teach transcend the realm of common human experience and acceptance. But we can only understand an abstract concept we do not know by associating it with something we do know in order to infer

---

14 *The Observer Part I*, February 20-24, 1998, Tape 376 ed. (Yelm: Ramtha Dialogues, 1998).

its meaning from that. Thus Ramtha borrows a multitude of words and imagery from different traditions familiar to us to express and explain his message.

> "Where did all this come from? Where did consciousness and energy come from? Now this is going to take a lot of focus because I am going to talk to you in terms that are very limited. I can only tell you words that you have pictures for. So as I teach you, your brain is firing the pictures. Your brain doesn't talk in words; it talks in holograms, pictures. So the language is really sounds to describe the true language, which is pictures. So now as I teach you this, I have chosen words to cause your brain to fire neurologically inner images, and those images then give you an idea, a visual, of where you came from. But remember that it is much more transcendent than this description. Do you understand? How many of you understand? So be it."[15]

Many times he borrows a concept but modifies and qualifies its meaning. The concept of God, for example, is the first one to be noted. As the great German idealists emphasized, "Before we can have a meaningful discussion about God, we need to define first what it is we mean by such term." Another important term he uses in a specific and unique way is "consciousness."

He also redefines the language he uses by coining new words. The meaning of these coined words becomes clear within the context of his teaching, and the particular teaching becomes clarified also by the use of such uncommon words.

Ramtha at a recent event made the comment that "Some things I cannot tell you, just because of the poverty of the language."[16]

---

15 *Ramtha: Creating Personal Reality*, Tape 380 ed. (Yelm: Ramtha Dialogues, 1998).
16 *Blue College Retreat*, March 5, 2000, Tape 443.4 ed. (Yelm: Ramtha Dialogues, 2000).

The Brain and the Creative Power of the Word

Furthermore, an integral part of Ramtha's system of thought is his unique understanding of how the brain processes consciousness and produces thoughts that are then translated into the abstractions we use for communication called words. Ramtha explains to a beginning group of students the following:

> "Consciousness and energy creates reality."
> "The brain is different than consciousness, although consciousness is what gives cells their life. The brain does not create consciousness; it creates thought."
> "Consciousness and energy is the Source. When it gives life, it gives life because of a thought. The body, the human body, contains a brain, that that brain is the vehicle for streams of consciousness and energy. It is its power source."
> "The brain's job is to take impulses of consciousness and energy at the neurological level — don't go to sleep — and create thoughts. The brain actually chops up the stream of consciousness into coherent thought-forms that are lodged in the neurosynaptic pathways in the brain."[17]

Words are the third generation in a stream of consciousness and energy picked up and frozen by the neurosynaptic connections of the brain that fire and translate them into holographic pictures we call thoughts. The ultimate meaning, the ontological aspect of words, then rests in the creative quality of consciousness and energy with which they are charged and from where they ultimately spring. The

---

17 *Beginning C&E® Workshop*, February 3-4, 1996, Tape 326 ed. (Yelm: Ramtha Dialogues, 1996).

creative or destructive and lasting quality of the spoken word is no longer considered anymore. Stories of magical incantations and vengeful curses are definitely out of fashion today and only appear in folklore, myth, and fantasy. But what is the truth behind these stories?

One of the greatest thinkers and one of the precursors of the Spanish Renaissance and the Spanish language, Fray Luis de León — who was professor at the University of Salamanca during the second half of the sixteenth century — taught theology to the famous Christian mystic St. John of the Cross and was a friend and editor of St. Theresa of Avila. All three of them were at once accused of heresy and judged by the Inquisition but, in the end, they survived their unjust charges. And they are recognized today as great examples and saints. Fray Luis de León developed a unique philosophy of names following the concepts of the Jewish and Christian mystics.

He explained in his philosophical work *De los Nombres de Cristo* that a term or name of something contains within it the very thing that it names. Thus he concluded that when we entertain such a name as a thought, we must somehow also possess the essence of the thing it names. For Fray Luis de León, the word was by no means mere convention and void of meaning. For him, they contained creative power; they contained consciousness and energy, using Ramtha's terminology.[18]

The ancient Hebrew language probably contains the clearest and closest interpretation of the word as creative consciousness and energy. The first book of the Jewish Torah, the book of Genesis, contains — as part of its opening word בראשית, "Barashith" — the word ברא, "Barah" (bêth, rêš, aleph). The second word of this same

---

18 Fray Luis de León, *De los Nombres de Cristo* (Spain: Colección Austral, Espasa Calpe, 1991).

book is "Barah" on its own. The word "Barah" refers to both a noun and a verb. As a singular noun it alludes to the root-word, as in ancient Aramaic and Syriac, for "a word," and as a verb it refers to the action of creation. This double meaning is by no means arbitrary, especially when we consider that the context of the book of Genesis is the story of creation. This book describes God creating the heavens and the earth in seven days through the power of his word and spoken command without the aid of any preexisting substance.

God is pictured *commanding* his creation into being and approving of it by *seeing* it as a very good deed. This context provides the term "Barah" with a very profound background which charges and qualifies it with meaning. A great part of Jewish mysticism and the Jewish and Christian Cabala of the Middle Ages was founded on the understanding that words and thoughts had a creative and divine quality. Words were the focus of meditation and the agents that brought the individual closer to the divine. In the light of these considerations, it is not difficult to find a parallel between the concept of "the creative power of *the word of God*" and "the creative power of *consciousness and energy*," thought, expressed in the word and effected into being.

An important difference between these two concepts though is that the only time the word has creative power, according to Genesis, is when it is used by God and not by men and women. In other words, it is considered a divine attribute. In Ramtha's understanding, the creative power of the word is available to everyone. For Ramtha, this important quality of humanity is a testament to the extent to which we have forgotten our divinity as well as the very foundations of our free will.

"So that the definition of God then, which comes down to the definition of you, is you are consciousness and energy, whatever your will lights upon. And why the seven seals? Because our will can work in any of these areas. And the body is an absolute duplicate map to that which is termed the seven kingdoms — as within, so without; as above, so below — and that what gives these kingdoms their viability and indeed their justice in being are our will and our choice. That is all. But that is everything. That is everything."

"Consciousness and energy is the intrinsic law — the only law, if we want to call it that — that is in action. And what it does, it is so unlimited that it supports it. It is the only law, if we want to call it that, that the will that you have could absolutely be free in."[19]

The law of consciousness and energy is always active in the person, although it may not always be apparent due to the level of awareness of the individual. Ramtha explains that people are commonly not aware of the true direction of their intent and focus, thus making them assume their will is not manifesting. People, on the other hand, who are mastering their human condition and becoming enlightened learn to become aware and redirect at will the underlying intent which creates their lives.

"Unless you understand consciousness and energy create reality, you will always have the sentences — but, why, I can't, it is too hard, failure, lack — you will always have all of those. And the wonder is that consciousness and energy is creating your objection."[20]

"Consciousness has no laws; whatever it is is the law. And that is the law, to make known the unknown.

---

19 *Walking the Journey of the Woman*, January 9, 2000, Tape 437.1 ed. (Yelm: Ramtha Dialogues, 2000).
20 Ibid.

> It has free rein. Energy is the handmaiden of thoughts. It is what collapses the subatomic world into particle reality and creates magnetic fields to draw what is already known into your bands. Everyone in our life reflects an aspect of who we are and that aspect is for an emotional redemption."[21]

Ramtha further explains that the mechanics of the law of consciousness and energy is expressed in the way language organizes verbs and nouns in a sentence. The verb is the action of consciousness and energy, and the noun represents the reality created by it. He concludes, therefore, that the verb should always go first in a sentence, followed by the noun, in order to truly emulate how reality is actually created. Ramtha's own native language had this structural format. Some ancient languages, like classical Greek, show signs of this format also.

It is important for the reader to take account of these considerations when reading the teachings of Ramtha, for in some instances it may seem at first that his use of the English language is rather archaic or unrefined. Ramtha is very careful and thorough in the presentation of his thought. Everything he does — every term he uses — has a specific meaning, purpose, and is consistent with, and representative of, the totality of his message. The main concern in preparing Ramtha's teachings for publication in printed form has been to render them as much as possible in the context and form in which they were delivered. Great care has been taken to avoid altering and changing the meaning of the teachings by taking them out of context or by even introducing a system of punctuation that would change the meaning. Nevertheless, we are aware that the human element of perception and

---

21 *Blue College Weekend*, January 7, 2000, Tape 437 ed. (Yelm: Ramtha Dialogues, 2000).

limited understanding is inevitable. The only way to ensure that the message will be delivered and received in its pristine beauty and originality is when it is embraced by the reader as a true paradigm for their life. Then it bears the fruits of truth and wisdom it promises.

> "I gave you a great deal, indeed, of information, and it is to be certain that my language was not always understandable and that became an excuse. I saw my words, as you term them, edited and transposed for the sake of continuity of thought. And yet when the words were edited for the sake of continuity of thought, the words that were left out were words of profound power. 'Indeed as it were in this time as you know it, unto this very hour, that which is termed indeed the God within you rise up, as it is so seen at this moment, to address that which is termed, as it were indeed, the deepening shadow that lies deep within the soul of all of that which is termed humanity.' Remember those words? They were left out for the sake of continuity.
>
> "Now the words were powerful because they were not mere words. They were arranged according to the address and the impact of their energy and how they would be destined to bloom. So words that I have used in your past were there deliberately for the empowerment of the moment. I was the one delivering them; therefore I was obligated to bring them into being."[22]

---

22 *Preserving Oneself*, February 6, 1991, Tape 304 ed. (Yelm: Ramtha Dialogues, 1991).

Summary: Ramtha's Teachings
As a Self-Contained System of Thought and
Interpretation of the Nature of Reality

Cornerstones of Ramtha's System of Thought

The Void, one vast nothing, all things potentially
Consciousness and energy create reality
Behold God! You are the forgotten Gods
Our purpose is to make known the unknown

Ramtha's teachings cover a vast amount of subjects, yet they all serve to expound the fundamental concepts of his own system of thought. On repeated occasions he emphasized that the totality of his message could be expressed in the statement, "You are God." But how are we to interpret this statement? There are probably as many definitions of the term "God" as there are people on the Earth. In order to understand Ramtha's teachings correctly, it is crucial that we become aware of both our own concept of God and how it stands in contrast with Ramtha's own explanation and definition of God and the nature of reality.

What is the essence of all things? What is their source? What is their nature? What is their destiny? Ramtha's approach to these questions begins with his concept of the Void. The Void is the source from which all that exists sprang. He describes the Void as "one vast nothing materially, yet all things potentially." In the Void there is nothing — neither movement nor action. Many philosophical approaches to the question of God, including the theologies of monotheistic religions, have conceived of God as an all-knowing, infinite, absolute, transcendent, and immutable being. In Ramtha's system, the attributes of absoluteness, infinity, and immutability are characteristics of the Void. The Void is self- contained, self-sufficient, in a state of rest, and of no need. Even though the Void is seen as an all-encompassing vastness, in its original state it contains no knowledge of itself, for knowledge is an action.

"All right. Let's go back before there was a beginning. Can you imagine this: If time then is based upon the concept that it exists between two points of consciousness — are you still with me, philosophically? — what was, when there wasn't two points of consciousness? Can you imagine that? Come on. Wake up. Now if there were not two points of consciousness, there was nothing. Do you know what the word 'nothing' means? No-thing. Can you imagine a vastness of no-things? Well, there was and still is.

"So here is what you are going to have a problem with. This condition always was. That is what you have problems with. You can't imagine something that existed that wasn't nothing and never had its own creator. It always was. That is what baffles the yellow brain.[23] Always was. Powerful. Well, we call this — and I want you to write it down — the Void. The Void. Now I want you to write the definition of the Void right after it. The Void is one vast nothing materially, all things potentially. So would you turn to your neighbor and read the definition of the Void.

"Now so we call the Void one vast nothing materially, yet all things potentially. Come on, beginners, say it. Now this is what in the elder days of my appearance here I called the Mother/Father Principle. It is called the Mother/Father Principle, the Void. It was also called the Source — the Source. Now there is a great, brilliant scientist who got an understanding of the Void. He kind

---

23 The "yellow brain" is Ramtha's description of the neocortex, the house of analytical and emotional thought.

of called it the ether but that is incorrect. This scientist understood — and his name is David Bohm — he understood that particles don't travel. They don't travel; they appear and reappear. What an amazing concept. Don't they do this? Yes, down here they do."

"He said the Void folds, enfolds, and outfolds potentials. He is right."[24]

The concept of God as creator, "first cause," and "unmoved mover" that we find in Aristotle's philosophy and Thomas Aquinas' theology is described by Ramtha in terms of the Void contemplating itself and knowing itself. This act of contemplation represents a unique movement in the Void that produced a point of awareness and knowingness of itself. This point of awareness is referred to as Point Zero, the Observer, primary consciousness, consciousness and energy, and God. Point Zero carries the primordial intent to make known and experience all that is unknown and in a state of potentiality within the vastness of the Void. This is the basis for evolution. The Void contemplating itself is the source and origin of the human person. Ramtha's statement, "You are God," refers to the person as the Observer, the embodiment of Point Zero, and creative consciousness and energy.

Point Zero fulfilled its nature to make known the unknown and evolve by imitating the act of contemplation of the Void. In doing this, Point Zero produced a reference point of awareness that served as a mirror through which it could become aware of itself. Ramtha refers to this mirror consciousness as secondary consciousness. Point Zero rests in the bosom of the Void and has no limits to what it can know. The reflection between Point Zero and the mirror consciousness is what produces an environment, a tangible

---

24 *Ramtha: Creating Personal Reality,* Tape 380 ed. (Yelm: Ramtha Dialogues, 1998).

plane of existence in time and space. The Spirit is the dynamic aspect of Point Zero. It is the will or intent that desires to know and experience the unknown. The exploration of the potentials of the Void by Point Zero and the mirror consciousness is what produced seven levels of consciousness and, correspondingly, seven levels of time and space, or frequency. This journey and act of creation down seven levels of consciousness and energy are referred to as the journey of involution. The journey back to God and the Void is called the journey of evolution. The soul is different from the Spirit. Ramtha speaks of the soul as the Book of Life. The soul is the recorder of all the experiences and the wisdom gained in the journey of involution and evolution.

The predicament of the human being is expressed in terms of forgetfulness, amnesia, and ignorance of its origins and destiny. The traveler, or mirror consciousness, identified itself so much with the densest and slowest plane of existence that it forgot its own immortality and divinity. Humanity has become a stranger to itself, to the God that lives within us and is us and searched for help, meaning, and redemption from an outside source. In doing this, humanity denies its own divinity and precludes any chance for liberation from its present condition.

It is important to note that in Ramtha's system of thought, the material world — the densest plane of existence — and the physical body are never regarded as evil, undesirable, or intrinsically bad. A dualistic interpretation of reality typically found in the gnostic traditions — emphasizing the struggle between good and evil, good and bad, light and darkness, sin and righteousness — is intrinsically excluded in Ramtha's system of thought. What becomes an undesirable condition is to remain in a state of ignorance and denial as to our true nature and destiny. It is absurd to argue for our limitations when we are, as consciousness and energy, the ones who created them.

The Great Work is the practical application of Ramtha's teachings where the person has the opportunity to know oneself and become enlightened. The path to enlightenment is the journey of evolution back to Point Zero. In accomplishing this task, the person fulfills the mandate to make known the unknown and bring to the Void its experience to be turned into perennial wisdom.

> "So of all of that which is termed the solar system and space and stars and nebulae and telstars, what is space? It is not what you see that dazzles the eye that is important but what it exists in, the nothing. What is that? The nothing, the Void. Could that be the progenitor of light and constellations and star systems and nebulae? It is. It is called the Void. What is the Void? It is that which exists without time, distance, and space."
>
> "Now the Ancient School then is based not on new truth but literally about that which is termed the foundations of the world: how the solar system was set into being and why, and who are you in relationship to the solar system; what is your journey, the solar system's journey; what indeed is the meaning of the cosmos; why are you so small in regard to the bigger picture? You are going to learn that in this school. And this is not new truth; this is old truth.
>
> "The school then is built upon a cornerstone. Think about the school as that which is termed a mammoth building that is nothing you can see but is everything you feel, and the cornerstone to this building is called consciousness and energy. So what did I say? Turn to your neighbor and tell them that. Consciousness and energy, it is the cornerstone of this school. Consciousness and energy, do you know what those

words mean? A dream with power and intent. That is what they mean. So the school is built starting with this cornerstone.

"And another cornerstone is that you are God. Will you say that. Louder. Now, see, you didn't get torched alive by saying that, did you? This is not blasphemy. This is the Holy Writ. Say it again. So be it. Now that is a wonderful place to be, but it does have some responsibilities. So the other cornerstone is that you are God. And what is the other stone? It makes the square. Consciousness and energy create reality. You are God.

"And what is the other stone if we are going to square this up? The other stone is that your life is to evolve what is already known. Will you say that. Again.

"Now does that mean that you are supposed to be like a busybody and go over to your neighbor and start evolving their life? Does it? It means tend to your own destiny. Your own destiny is your life. And you are to see what you created, what you are emotionally clinging to, own that emotion, and go about creating new paradigms of life. And if you do that, you will never die; you won't end up in the graveyard. So the more that you create, the younger you become. The younger you become, the older you become. So is it possible that you could never run out of ideas? Yes. Will you turn to your neighbor and tell them that. Come on. Come on. We want this manifestation. Come on."[25]

"And the evidence is the truth that says that you have not even begun to dream your greater dreams or to live them. And how do we know that? Because look at this: You use less than a tenth of this brain, less than a tenth."[26]

All of the disciplines of the Great Work designed and used by Ramtha to initiate his students into the teachings are modeled according to, and imitate in some way, the process of

---

25 *Ramtha: Creating Personal Reality,* Tape 380 ed. (Yelm: Ramtha Dialogues, 1998).
26 Ibid.

the Void contemplating itself, which gave birth to consciousness and energy, which in turn create the nature of reality.

In conclusion, the four cornerstones of Ramtha's philosophy are the concept of the Void, consciousness and energy creating seven levels of reality, the statement "You are God," and the mandate to make known the unknown. There are many traces of Ramtha's thought found in ancient traditions, although in most cases all that remains are faint echoes that have barely survived the passing of time and the loss of their appropriate context for interpretation. Some of these traditions are the philosophies of the ancient Egyptians and Pharaoh Akhnaton, Zarathustra, Buddha's description of himself as the awakened, Socrates' understanding of virtue and the immortality of the soul, Plato's concept of universal forms, Yeshua ben Joseph's life and teachings, the works of St. Thomas the Apostle, the *Hymn of the Pearl,* the hymn to the divine word in the Gospel according to John, Apollonius of Tyana, Origen, Mani, the Cathars and Albigenses, Francis of Assisi, the Jewish and Christian mystics, John of the Cross's sketch of the *Ascent of Mount Carmel,* where the apex is placed at the top of the head of the human body, the works of art of various artists like Michelangelo and Leonardo da Vinci, the writings and mystical experiences of Theresa of Avila, the works of Fray Luis de León, the humanists of the Renaissance movement in Europe, the Rosicrucians, the masters of the Far East, and others.

Finally, it is important to note that a common element in Ramtha's presentation of his teachings is his reinterpretation of the traditional understanding of the life and teachings of Yeshua ben Joseph.[27] He repeatedly quotes

---

27 Ramtha refers to Jesus Christ by the name Yeshua ben Joseph, following the Jewish tradition of the era.

from this source but in a way that throws new light and insight on Jesus' teachings. Ramtha's particular interpretation of Jesus is far from an arbitrary manipulation of information. Whenever Ramtha diverts from the traditional understanding of Jesus' life and teachings, he provides substantial evidence for his statements and assumptions.

We would like to end this introductory essay by noting the parallels between Jesus' prayer — the Lord's Prayer found in the synoptic Gospels — and the prayer of Ramtha to the Spirit, which bears great similarities to it. The Lord's Prayer is the traditional prayer in Christianity used to address God. This prayer is regarded as being representative of Jesus' teachings. On the other hand, Ramtha's prayer to the Spirit offers his students the means to enact and proclaim the basic affirmations of his teachings. This prayer is a powerful initiation into the sacred mysteries of creation, the Spirit, and the journey of involution and evolution back to God.

*Parallel between Jesus' Prayer to the Father and
Ramtha's Prayer to Our Spirit*

THE LORD'S PRAYER	RAMTHA'S PRAYER
"Our Father	"O my beloved Spirit,
	my mighty Spirit,
	Omnipotent One,
	you who are filled
	with the power of
in heaven,	heaven and Earth,
may your name be held holy,	fill me with your power.
	O my Spirit, fill me
your kingdom come,	with your manifested kingdom,
your will be done,	that I may be a vessel
	to bring forth
on Earth as in heaven.	that which is unseen in heaven,
	to subdue that which is seen
	on Earth.
Give us today	Manifest for me
our daily bread	my daily food,
	that I may live
and forgive us	to know my guilt,
our debts,	my doubt,
as we have forgiven those	my sorrow,
who are in debt to us.	and then realize the truth.
	O mighty Spirit,
And do not put us	do not allow me
to the test,	to be tempted.
but save us	Protect me
from the evil one."[28]	from all that would persuade me.
	And manifest through me
	God divine.
	So say I.
	So be it.
Amen	To life."[29]

28 Matt. 6:9-13 New Jerusalem Bible.
29 *Our Omnipotent Spirit: Direct Line to the Power of Manifestation*, February 23, 1996,
Tape 327.09 ed. (Yelm: Ramtha Dialogues, 1996).

Those terms in Ramtha's prayer that find a clear parallel to the prayer of Jesus could serve as a key for the interpretation of Jesus' message. We find that when we apply Ramtha's understanding of these terms to the teachings of Jesus, his message is in striking agreement to the works attributed to Thomas the Apostle in the Nag Hammadi collection.[30] This is important since the works of Thomas have been placed in the mid-first century, a date prior to the Gospel of John and the synoptic Gospels themselves.

> "Now I want you to also know that if you feel slightly repelled from this prayer, it is more than likely from a deep conscious memory of religion and your distaste for it. But listen to me. This was known in times of antiquity. The great, great masters and Christs of the Earth dispatched this knowledge to people. Fragments of the sacred mysteries were stolen and around them were created a religion in which a great travesty happened. And the great travesty is that religion became the caretaker of God and indeed ultimately had power over all of its parishioners' souls. Furthermore, they took this knowledge and said that only by Christ can this happen. That is not true. Furthermore, they are talking about a deity that they have taught exists extraneously from the people. That is not true.
>
> "Notice in this prayer we are saying, 'O my beloved Spirit.' We are giving back to God God's ultimate plan

---

30 "In this book I shall first argue that in no meaningful historical sense is Thomas 'Gnostic.' Whatever the Gnostics of the Apocryphon of John, the Origin of the World, Eugnostos, Pistis Sophia, etc., were doing, the Gospel of Thomas is doing something else. If one would like to see what a Gnostic Sayings Gospel does look like, one should turn to the Gospel of Philip. Then I shall show that although Thomas is by no means a systematic document, it does have a comprehensible set of ideas, which are, for the most part, drawn from the Jewish Wisdom and apocalyptic traditions. Finally, I shall place Thomas in its context in the very early church. It is a collection of sayings used to instruct newly-baptized Christians. It appears to reflect an early form of Johannine preaching and probably came into being at about the same time as the Q document (the sayings source from which many scholars

and power for ourselves, where it should be. We are invoking the deity and its power within us. We are the projection of that deity, given a will to create. When we evoke it, we evoke it from our own deep and superb place. This is not a religious prayer. It is the evoking prayer of individual Spirit, Almighty God — Almighty God."[31]

Ramtha's prayer contains the basic elements of his philosophy. The prayer is addressed to our personal Spirit, the dynamic aspect of Point Zero, the God within the person rather than to a being outside and transcendent of ourselves. Our personal Spirit is described as the Almighty and Omnipotent One, the offspring of the Void itself. The concept of heaven is interpreted in terms of the sea of potentials of the Void. The "earth" is used in reference to the manifestation and expression of these potentials. Heaven is the creative principle of consciousness and energy, and the Earth is its sevenfold manifestation and expression.

The human personality — secondary consciousness or mirror consciousness — is the one addressing the prayer to the Observer, or primary consciousness. It expresses its desire to become a vessel of unseen potentials, to make known the unknown. The value in feeding the physical body and sustaining a human form of life is to have the opportunity to

---

believe Matthew and Luke drew much of their material). Thomas should be dated ca. ~A.D. 50—70."

"If these conclusions are accepted, then the Gospel of Thomas can take a place in scholarship and in Christian self-understanding which it is now denied. I am less concerned that any specific conclusions I draw about the meaning of Thomas be accepted than that the text be accorded a place in the mid-first century, for only then will the question of the meaning of Thomas for Christian history be re-opened." Stevan L. Davies, *The Gospel of Thomas and Christian Wisdom* (New York: Seabury Press, 1983), p. 2.

31 *Our Omnipotent Spirit: Direct Line to the Power of Manifestation*, February 23, 1996, Tape 327.09 ed. (Yelm: Ramtha Dialogues, 1996).

become aware of our guilt, doubt, and sorrow. In other words, what is important in life is to release and own the truth of all those human emotions that keep us repeating the experiences of our past. The soul provides the agenda of what still needs to be resolved in our lives in order to continue our journey of evolution back to God. The goal of the prayer is the achievement of unity with the divine, the attainment of enlightenment. To manifest God divine through the individual is to become God/woman, God/man realized, an immortal being no longer limited by time or space. The closing statement of the prayer distinguishes it from being a mere petition to be granted by an external source or a superior being. This prayer is rather a powerful command to manifest and a bold recognition of the creative power of the human person as the Observer and a God.

The teachings of Ramtha offer us a unique perspective from which to view the mystery of life. They offer us a framework in which the questions that have remained unanswered by philosophy, science, and religion find a new meaning. These teachings can broaden the scope of human experience far beyond the boundaries set by science and the various religions of the world to this day. Ramtha's system of thought is neither a religion nor a philosophical interpretation of reality. It is the truth that was gained and verified by the experience of a member of the human race. In this sense it is Ramtha's knowledge, Ramtha's science. And now that the path has been trodden upon, the doors are open for those who desire to explore it and make their own journey into the unknown.

Jaime F. Leal Anaya
March 16, 2000

PART I

RAMTHA,
A MASTER'S JOURNEY TO
ENLIGHTENMENT

CHAPTER ONE
Ramtha's Autobiography

Lemuria and Atlantis

I am Ramtha the Enlightened One. I was known as Ram. I was the first conqueror this plane ever knew. I conquered three-quarters of your known world, entity. My march lasted for sixty-three years. I ascended on the northeast side of the Indus River in front of my complement, entity, that was two million strong. My peoples now make up the populace of Indus, Tibet, Nepal, as it were indeed, and even that which is termed southern Mongolia. My peoples are a mixture, as it were indeed, of Lemurians, of that which is termed Ionians — later to be that which is termed Macedonia — and their color, as it were indeed, mixed with that which is termed the tribespeople, that which is termed, as it were indeed, the tribal peoples escaping from that which is termed Atlatia. My blood, entity, is in all of them.

Of the entirety of that which is termed the continent Atlatia, I was not a traveler upon it, only unto that which is called the southernmost port called Onai. There was a canal, as it were indeed, what you term canal or waterway, that connected that which is termed indeed Atlatia with that which is called Mu. You understand what Mu means, Lemuria? The greatest motherland of them all. Truly that was the cradle of civilization, if man wishes to find where it was.

But in the waterway, as it were indeed, the pilgrimage that were making their advent unto that which is called Atlatia at that time were doing so, as it were indeed, for the land called Mu was overrun with that which is termed the great beasts.[1] They were remnants, as it were indeed, of a further creativity that I have explained to you in that which is termed creation.[2] And there were many of the peoples, as it were indeed, all their structures were underground, you see. None in Lemuria, as it were indeed, had structures that lived above the ground. They either lived in that which is called the mount — And there was only one great mountain range, and that be, as it were indeed, into the upper Pacific coast of this your country into that which is called the waterways. In that particular time they made, as it were indeed, their hovels in the mountains. But into the great flatlands, as it were, the great plain of Mu, all lived underground. Thus they had a wonderful network of tunnels indeed, highways and byways, as they are so termed indeed, that was beneath the ground for the mere safety of that which is termed indeed the animals above. The animals, as it were indeed, became, as it were indeed, more rampant, producing, as it were indeed, better and bigger, as it were indeed, enormous creatures.

The entities, as it were indeed, that decided to stay with the motherland knew that the land was going to be going down, as it were, for the great waters already, as it were indeed, were beginning to form in the stratum. And when the land went down, as it were indeed, in its surface, it did so for the destruction of that which is termed indeed the animals and the beasts. And when it did, that which is termed the continent shifted upon its rotating axis and gave unto the

---

1 The dinosaurs.

2 *Creation*, Specialty Tape 005 ed. (Yelm: Ramtha Dialogues, 1980). See also *A Master's Reflection on the History of Humanity*. Part I, *Human Civilization, Origins and Evolution* (Yelm: JZK Publishing, a division of JZK, Inc., 2001).

higher regions of Lemuria a great freeze. The freeze, as it were indeed, finished them off. Before, as it were indeed, the land was going under, those, as it were indeed, the old fathers of Lemuria, chose to stay with their beloved land and go with it. They remembered the time of their advent, you know. It is told in their history, as it were. The younger ones made their pilgrimage, as it were indeed, to Atlatia. And the one waterway that connected Atlatia, as it were indeed, unto Lemuria was a canal place.

We were called slaves, dogs, soulless, mindless. All, as it were indeed, that came from that continent were not loved and honored by the Atlatians for they were high in their intellect while the Lemurians, as it were indeed, were strong in that which is termed the Spirit, the invisible understanding. My forefathers worshiped a power that they called the Unknown God, and even late unto your history his name remained on altars, as it were indeed, throughout various civilizations.

When I came unto that which is called Atlatia, I came through that which is termed a canal, and the greatest port in Atlatia, as it were indeed, was its southern sphere called Onai. And you think this city to be great?[3] Onai's, as it were indeed, port land would have made two of this great city along with its coast. It was enormous. The bowl, or what they call a bowl, that separated, as it were indeed, the Atlatians from the Lemurians was rather a swamp area and it bowled in the center; thus it had, as it were indeed, some waters within it. But the swampland, as it were indeed, was a most immobile place. And not even that which is termed outlaws, by my beloved physician, would tread into that which is now called your America. And it separated the two continents in understanding.

---

3 Ramtha is referring to New York City where this particular dialogue took place.

Atlatia at that time, as it were indeed, it was a great continent of a civilization that had perfected the thought into that which is called the power of pure energy. They, as it were indeed, worshiped the intellect. That is why, as it were indeed, on this part of your country, in this that you call your Americas, that that of the eastern coastline is known for its intellect and that of the western is known for its Spirit. It is a truth. It is a lingering attitude that is here. The very coastline here of your great city indeed was that which is termed indeed a coastline in even farther islands from the northern part of Atlatia. Thus that which you call the Americas, they are called Brazil — is that a good name? — and South America, they used to be like this. They were one landmass and they formed into a point, and when the point formed, all the landmass that went up from that was the greater continent called Atlatia. And what separated Atlatia from these two landmasses was the canal zone that connected Lemuria to it. It was a singular waterway. It was the only port that the southern sphere of Onai had.

The Cataclysm

Now you say, "Where, Ramtha, were all of the waters, the oceans that we have?" They were still in your stratum. The water has always been in your stratum. That is what made the wondrous child called Terra fertile, for it took the sunlight, as it were indeed, and evenly deposited it all over, as it were indeed, the Earth. How did the great freeze come about, as it were indeed, in the final days? When the waters came down, as it were indeed, to the great waterway, when that which is termed indeed light had been perfected by that which is termed indeed the Atlatians for the purpose of travel, for the purpose of destruction, for the purpose of transmuting, as it were indeed, thoughts and things, the great light, as it were indeed, severed the great waterway in the stratum. It was there, as it were indeed, that the water began to fall into that which is called an atmospheric understanding or what you term moisture.

Little bit by little bit, as it were indeed, as this began, that which is called indeed Lemuria began to rumble, as it were indeed, within its bowels and quake, as it were indeed. And as it began to quake, indeed the stratum that had been pierced by the great light indeed above Lemuria began to flood, as it were indeed, with water. As the water came down, as it were indeed, upon the Lemurians, the Earth, as it were indeed, began to tilt, for it is like when the babe is in the womb and if you puncture the womb, as it were indeed, and the water that is in the womb that protects the babe, it will throw the babe, as it were indeed, to one side, for the babe is balanced in the womb according to the water, the same as it be, as it were indeed, with Terra.

When the waters came down, as it were indeed, upon the great planet, the planet, as it were indeed, shifted to the point, as it were indeed, of a great coldness, for when it shifted and the hole was in the stratum, as it were indeed, that which is termed sunlight, as it were, was taken, condensed all around where the stratum was still, and there was no warmth coming through, as it were indeed, the punctured hole, thus creating the great freeze. It was all immaculately done, for it destroyed Lemuria, that which they termed dogs, as it were indeed, no-things, and all the animals which were beginning to pose a threat, as it were indeed, to the Atlatians.

Now what happened to Atlatia, as it were indeed, when the great tumbling, as it were indeed, and catastrophe, as you term it, of Lemuria began to fall? It began to fall in sections. It was the northern part of Lemuria that went under first, and when it went under from the freeze, the waterways came. The great water began to fill in each part as the continent began to shelve itself lower. As it began to do this indeed, that which is termed indeed the continents that set themselves together that were the supportive elements of Atlantis began to move apart, for the water came in through the waterway, as it were indeed, and began to cleave a waterway that separated the continents, and they began to move. That which you term indeed the continents Brazilian and that which is called your southern Americas, as it were indeed, are separate parts that once were together, where now a great waterway flows.

You see, the Atlatians fervently believed that this was an act of their intelligence, for they were world conquerors, for their terrible light, as it were indeed, was not terrible at all. It was merely what you term lasers but in a more refined state, usable state. They of themselves, as it were indeed, despised the pilgrims, or those that had no intellect into machines. Once, as it were indeed, they saw the crumbling from afar and saw, as it were indeed, the stratum splitting, they were so arrogant as to believe, as it were indeed, that their annihilation would never be and that the hole, as it were indeed, into the stratum was only an adventure to them.

So the continent Atlantis — it was referred to as Atlatia — it is and was the red civilization. What you term your Indians, your red people, are, as it were indeed, the ancients known, as it were indeed, as Atlatians.

Pilgrimage to Onai

Now during my time when the pilgrimage, as it were indeed, was set and there would be that which is termed slums in Onai, it took a long time, as it were indeed, from this that I have told you to take into proper operation. The time, as it were indeed, from the first stratum pierce, as it were indeed, and to the canal, as it were, raising itself and splitting itself took that which is termed indeed six hundred years in your time to do. It is a long time; not in a moment.

When all the pilgrims, as it were indeed, were at the southern sphere of Atlantis during that time, as it were indeed, the advent of the technological understanding had already come to a great ebb, and already, as it were indeed, the northern parts of Atlantis were beginning to crumble and to fall under, for they were misusing their light. You see, they could travel upon the light. Their aeroships traveled on the light. They could not go around, for the light was not, as it were indeed, round in form; it followed a straight line. They wanted to go up. And they put their aeroships on the light and they went up, and they broke the stratum when they did so. And when they broke the stratum, as it were indeed, into the northern sphere, there came the great waters. And when the waters came, as it were indeed, there was a great crumbling. Great pressure was emitted upon that which is termed Terra. And the northern part which sits off of your eastern line here, as it were, began to fall and to crack and to ebb, as it were indeed, as great mountains break up and fall, as it were indeed, under the gust of waves. That is what it appeared to do. Not to be, as it were indeed, forewarned, they continued, as it were indeed, though their landmass was falling into water, to go straight up.

There is a saying in your Book of Books that is written that was most appropriate for this time, and the saying said, "Behold, in their last days they thrust themselves as eagles to plant their nests amongst the stars, and I brought them down."[4] That was for them. That is not the future; that was the past. And when, as it were indeed, they kept doing so, they kept breaking the stratum more. And behold, as it were indeed, that which was under the Earth, the light, as it were indeed, began to surface itself where the breaking of the stratum had appeared. And all of that which is termed indeed the water that remained in the outer stratum that was now under what you call your equator, that enveloped the bottom of Terra, as it were indeed, became rigid, for no longer was there a consistency even in the water to carry the light evenly to have warmth emitted. It was now displaced. One by one this continent broke up and went under.

I came unto Atlatia, as it were indeed, in what is called the last hundred years. And in the last hundred years, as it were indeed, as to what you call, as it were indeed, your Carolinas, as they are so properly termed, the continent had been broken up under them — they are remnants of mountaintops — all the way down.

The civilization of the Atlatians at that particular point had degenerated itself into tyrants, tyrants who no longer knew how to use the technological advances that their forefathers had used but of power through thought. The tyrants formed democracies. In the democracies the tyrants, who governed the people through irreputable law, not a republic — In a democracy of irreputable law, as it were indeed, we, that which

4 "Though you soar aloft like the eagle, though your nest is set among the stars, thence I will bring you down, says the Lord." Obadiah, chapter 1:4, The Bible, Revised Standard Version.

is termed indeed the Lemurians, the slums, the pilgrims, as it were indeed, the dogs, the no-things, the soulless, mindless waste of intellect, were being put to it. And that was my time. We did not have the great lights any longer. The great lights had been brought under, as it were indeed, when the last great quaking of Atlantis occurred, as it were indeed, in the center of its metropolis of science, and all was destroyed from there.

There is a place, as it were indeed, that is called the Dead Horse Drones.[5] It lies in your sea off, as it were, your eastern coast. Do you know there is no wind there? There have been mariners sail into that awful, devilish place and the wind is no more and they perish there. It is there, because there is no wind there, where, as it were indeed, the scientific center of that which is termed indeed Atlantis thus rests. And from that there is also a great door. It is controlled by that which is termed a great column or vacuum that leads into the inner civilization within your Earth.[6] Why is it dead there? You see, the attitude that was gathered up in the latter part of the days, the mediocrity of supreme intelligence in those latter days, emits still an attitude, as it were indeed, of sovereignty over all things. That is why there is no life there.

Now the day of the Ram, as it were indeed, when I was a little boy, it was not governed any longer by light but by tyrants, irreputable law, and human life was nothing. Your red

---

5 The Sargasso Sea, located between 20° to 35° North Latitude and 30° to 70° West Longitude. Currents in the Sargasso Sea are mostly dead calm. It is surrounded by some of the strongest currents in the world that interlock and isolate it completely, like the eye of a hurricane, from the rest of the Atlantic. Anything that drifts into its surrounding currents finds itself caught in the Sargasso Sea with little possibility for escape. This region, closely associated with the Bermuda Triangle, runs through what sailors traditionally call the Horse Latitudes because stalled ships, relying solely on wind power in the past, threw their horses and cattle overboard as a last resort to save on food and water.

6 See "Life in the Center of the Earth," Chapter 2 in *A Master's Reflection on the History of Humanity*. Part II, *Rediscovering the Pearl of Ancient Wisdom* (Yelm: JZK Publishing, a division of JZK, Inc., 2002).

men, your Indians, why were they slaughtered? For once they were the ones who slaughtered the white peoples, for they were once grand sovereigns of the entirety of Terra and for them, as it were indeed, their karma has come full circle. And in the land they called the waste to which they would put all vile and dung-heaps of dead in this maze that connected the two continents of swamp and no land. Have you ever tried to fix a growing thing in a land that is always wet? That is where your rice came from and the science of raising it came from, from your yellow peoples, for that was their meager homeland due to that which is called the Atlatians.

Now in my time all I had to deal with were tyrants. Is that not enough? Is that more powerful than the light? Indeed it is. And in my time, as it were indeed, beloved entity, they were direful times, for life was no-thing. It was nothing, as it were indeed, for one to pass a starving woman on the road and all put, as it were indeed, kerchiefs of fine linen that were delved into jasmine and rose water upon their noses, you see, as they walked by us. We were stinking, wretched things. And that is when I was born.

There was a time in my obedience and in my learning that I was a waif of sorts. I was tender in the frailness of my bodily movement. I had not, as it were indeed, strength to bring in the kindling, as it were indeed, for the brazier. Why was I this way, for I had not that which is nourishment to eat, I had not that which is called linens and furs to warm me when the winter and the silentness of the whiteness came forth? I had not these things; thus I was withered in bodily form.

When I was a little boy, indeed very small, that which is termed the illusions of my times were very destitute. You have created in this your time-flow a paradise because of that which is termed previous lives have taught you emotionally to create a more conducive consciousness in which you can expand in.

And when I was a little boy, that which is termed life and its illusion was very arduous indeed, for unto that which is termed my lineage 'twas that which is termed the dung of the earth. It was a waste of the Earth. In our conscious view of more prominent races, my people and their lineage would have been better to go down with the whole lot of the seas that slaughtered the great animals that lived on top of my land.

Contemplate you for a moment being termed worthless, soulless, no-use-of, disgusting, revolting, vile, that you would tolerate being spat on, urinated on, dung on you and not allowed to wash it away, only with your tears. Contemplate you motherless, fatherless. Indeed contemplate you the dog in the street to have a greater nourishment than you who salivate and hunger for only something to kill the agony in your belly. Contemplate you what sort of a dream be I in? The beginning of that which is termed the creation of man in his advent into his arrogant stupidity of intelligence, when so superb became he that anything less than the color of his skin or the cartouche upon his door was nothing, for there was nothing to equal his arrogance. That was my dream.

Before His Physical Incarnation

Who chose to be Ramtha? I. Who has chosen to be you? You. You, like I, before entering into that which is termed coagulated thought to what flesh is, chose the genetic patterns to which you would evolve from in your processes of understanding matter. When you are in the greater level and you have never descended into the lower frequencies, you cannot understand. In the innocence of your being you have no knowledge to understand. Thus you do not understand the whole of God's kingdom; you are simply there.

I did not create my body. I was left, as it were indeed, with that which is called the Atrium of the Constants. The Atrium of the Constants, as it were indeed, was a shelf. It was called the mantle of Terra. And in the mantle of Terra, as it were indeed, after the five races had made their descent upon the planes, as it were indeed, I was one who had not descended into the planes, that there was a whole mass that were with me. It was not unusual, for who was going to be there, master, when copulation began to spur itself and the fruitful seed began? What soul and Spirit were going to inhabit the seed if God had split himself into the two in order to make, as it were indeed, an extension of himself into creativity for his beloved brethren? He would not become the other brethren, as it were indeed, that he had created from the two; he could not. The child that is created from the two has to have a soul and a Spirit. Bodies are easily made; souls and Spirits are forever. It was through the bodily movement, as it were indeed, that I desired to come through to express. Why not?

I had been, as it were indeed, in many ways a foolhardy God, as all were foolhardy Gods, as it were indeed, in our beginnings, and misused our thoughts and our understandings to a competitiveness that destroyed a wondrous place. And I was amongst them, as it were indeed, as you were amongst them. And why do we want to express in the things that we create? If we do not express into the reality, how know we the reality exists? How know we the creativity of what we have done had an existence until we have become a part of it?

And when that which is termed indeed the races of man were blooming and fostering unto itself, as it were indeed, life and culture and love in the exuberance of God loving himself, it was in a natural order of events, as it were indeed, that I had my choice to come — as all in the Atrium or the mantle did — and I chose to come. I favored Terra, you see. I favored Terra, for Terra was a hope to us. It was beautiful, luminous, virtuous, and we had learned from our erroneous errors of our past. I wished to be a participant in it.

You see, what I did not know is that once you lower your vibrations to yet lower fields, you forget the higher fields, for you are living in the lower. When anyone born, as it were indeed, from the Atrium onto this plane forgot the higher, it was in their instincts. As animals have their instincts, man has his also, but not in a complete memory, as it were. The moment the Spirit takes in rapture the completeness of the body, Spirit, as it were indeed, has the totality of memory but ego does not.

Thus, as it were indeed, when upon being upon this plane, I was born an ignorant barbarian. You see, how could I comprehend what ignorance and the separation of the species — whether one be a barbarian or whether one be a king — how would I know what the difference of those attitudes were? To me, I could not define them, for I had not been them. You see, higher elements never judge lower elements, only lower elements judge the higher, because the higher hath not the capacity to understand the lower element, for it is not the lower element. You see what I say?

Before I entered I did not understand that man was enslaved to man. I did not understand, as it were indeed, of a waste called human life. Deprivation, enslavement, how could I understand those things? I was not those things, you see. And it wasn't until, as it were indeed, I became who I was was I at the mercy indeed of being ignorant, being a barbarian, a soulless, mindless — let us see — dog. You see, that is what we were considered. How did I know that that means that I was to be lower than the aristocracy, indeed that was called Atlatia, until I had been the victim of it?

When you are ignorant and you do not possess the common intellect of the land, then you are, as it were indeed, what is called riding on the outskirts of a society that does not accept you, for if they do, it reminds them perhaps of their own failing, you see. Ego does not like that. Altered ego does not like to be reminded it is altered.

I chose to be Ramtha. You chose to be you, your parents, the color of your skin, your gender determined by your soul, and where you live, what you would call a geographical area; correct? So you are you. In my life I was Ramtha, but into what Ramtha could be conceived, I was only the image of my greaters and never seen by my lessers. And the image of the greaters bestowed upon me disdainment, unliked, unloved, worthless, vile of the earth. Thus that was my image, to see what be I. And yet that which is termed the lineage and the line, genetically speaking, that I had chosen to come forth in were grand in their knowingness of unseen values. And they held onto them, even unto their motherland, which now sits beneath the great sea. And those pilgrims, as it were indeed, held onto a knowingness that my superiors would not believe unless it was put into reality, what you call machines, kingdoms, power, order.

My lineage I chose because I issued forth from the house called Ramuste, Ram. In that house — the house is designated from soul emotion collectively — and the house's, to which I issued forth from, emotional understanding was the power to master. There were those, as it were indeed, issued from houses of emotional creativity. They created that which is termed the machines, order, tyranny, segregation, hatred, but they were in the order to create progress. When you issue from a house, it is clear for you to know which one. All you have to do is turn your eyes inward to find out where your honor lies and to what allegiance it is. I don't need to tell you; you already know. And from this I chose to issue forth into what you would call Lemurians, Mu, against progress.

I did not blame my mother that I had no father, nor did I blame that which is termed my brother that our fathers were not of the same kin. I did not blame my mother for our absolute poverty. I did not blame that which is termed my God for what I had chosen openly to be. That is very much needed for you to learn, entities. But what occurred from a house of emotion to master versus a house of progress and what it led up to, it became combat. Combat, know you what the term is? You do not have to be in that which is termed, as it were indeed, a great army to know combat. All you have to have is a very sharp tongue.

Battle against the Unknown God

In my life, a little boy, I watched my mother being taken into the streets and her sweetness taken from her. I watched in my life, as it were, of where we lived and the despise that was around me. And I watched when my mother was taken. I watched the child grow inside of her belly and knew who it was. And I watched my mother weep. Why? That was very obvious. Would there be another sibling in the street to suffer as she had suffered in this promised land? I watched and helped my mother bring forth that which have been termed a little sistren in your language to life. I helped my mother because she was too weak to bear the child herself. And the little girl came forth yelling into the world. It wasn't happy. It was very obvious. But grave upon my being was that of my motheren's being, for weakened so was she that to the infant that sucked at her tender breast there was no milk, for she had starved, as it were indeed. And my sistren that was suckling at my mother's breast grew very weak.

Why, say you, we have this in our life, for we are the peasants, we are the nonessentials, we are the no-entities of a governed land? Who governed this land? Those of means, who had all of us live about their lands and run their fields and say they would not grant us even a stalk for our own bidding. And what, say you, did they with these things? They locked them into granaries and, lo, they fed themselves, their fastidious fingers upon their fastidious faces. I say unto you this was injustice. And who be this God they have spoken of? I am angered, for my mother weeps for there is no milk in her breast.

I scrounged in the street and slayed dogs and wildfowl and stole that which is termed, as it were indeed, the grain from the proprietors late in the evening, for I was very deft on my feet. And I fed my mother, who in turn suckled my little sister.

I did not blame my little sister for the death that would soon follow of my beloved mother, for the little girl suckled from my mother all of her strength. It was all given to new life, that new life could continue forth. And my mother perished with the babe at her breast. There was nothing; there was no more. And the little girl, as it were, became that which is termed diarrhetic. She could not hold what was coming into her body and passed it quickly from her body and lost all of the life in her body. So they were gone.

And as a little boy I gathered up that which is termed, as it were indeed, timbers and I laid them together. And I laid the timbers on top of my motheren and then stole away in the night and gathered that which is termed fire. And I brought it and coddled it, and I said a great prayer to my motheren and little sistren, and I loved them greatly. And I lit that which is termed the timbers, for if I did not do so swiftly, the stench from them would cause agitation in the area to which they lived and they would fling them into the desert, that the hyenas could prey upon them and tear them apart so that they are not bothered. I set them to fire and burned them.

My hate for the red peoples — they are called Atlatians — was increased into my being like a great viper only as a little boy. And there was nothing left, for my brothren was taken into subserviency into another city at the prey of a man, as it were indeed, and his needs for what is called loin gratification.

My lineage worshiped and loved that which was beyond the stars, beyond your moon. They loved what could not be identified. It was called the Unknown God. As a little boy I did not blame the Unknown God for his inability to love myself and my peoples and my motheren and little sistren. I did not blame him. I hated him.

And in my times no one died nobly of my peoples. There was no such thing as nobleness, virtuous, indeed. So I found a great mountain that loomed in the distance, a very mysterious place, for if I could climb there I would get in touch with the Unknown God out here and proclaim my hatred for him at his unfairness. So I began my journey.

I run from that of my hovel and there be a great mountain in a distance I barely see. And my journey, as it were indeed, hath been of ninety days — of ninety days, as it were indeed, of devouring locusts and roots and urnments of ants — did I find this mountain, for if there be a God, he would live there above all of us, as those who governed our land lived above us. And, lo, I sought him out, yet he was not there, except for the great cold. And I wept heartily until the whiteness, as it were indeed, iced itself from my tears. "I am a man. Why hath I not the dignity of one?"

Behold, there came unto me a sweet maiden as you have not seen, whose gilded hairs danced about her. The crown that be upon her hair was not of lilies or rosebuds or irises but an unknown flower. Her drapery, indeed her gowns, were translucent, mellow, and free. She came unto me and gave me a great sword. It sang. It sang. Yet it took nine hands to hold its handle, it was so great. And she gave it unto me.

This is what she said. "O Ram, O Ram, I beseech you who have learned — and woken of Spirit of the pity of our beings — the truth. There must be a truth that lingers in the land. Thus your prayers have been heard. And you are a man of means and conviction. Take you this sword and wear it well." And she was gone with herself. And I was blinded in my madness and my illusions in what I had seen. And no longer have I shivered against the great cold, but I found warmth there. And thus when I looked again where my tears had iced themselves, there grew a flower of such sweet refrain and color that I knew the flower, as it were indeed, would be that of what is termed hope.

The sword Crosham, the Winged Carrier, it was the Isness formulated itself into an apparition of the most beautiful sort, that gave me a sword and told me, "Go and conquer yourself." And the rest is history, so to speak. There is no entity that is in that which is termed a singular form that exists that gave me that sword. It is the harmony of the Isness that produced the Winged Carrier.

I came down from the mount with my great sword to the hovel of my mother, who had perished. Who was the suckling upon my mother's breast? It was you, for you are of my kingdom and my house and my dream. And you, as it were indeed, were saved, as it were, by the famine, for they opened their doors when I entered therein, and no longer weak of bodily movement or frail, that I was a Ram in all the sense of the word.

For that which is termed the rest of the story, there are a lot of you that know it well. But what drove me to conquer and to master, which was a part of my soul emotion, was the desire to make it even. I created war, indeed, for there were no warring factions against the arrogance of the Atlatians, none. I created it. I came from the great mountain, intimidated by the Unknown God, given a sword, and told then to conquer myself. I could not turn the blade around and hack my head off; it was too long. My arms would not reach, as it were indeed, to that which is called the stifle[7] of the sword. But I wept a great deal. But I got honor in my sword, and when I returned I laid siege to Onai.

The Great March against Tyranny

After we had laid siege to Onai, it took that which is termed a long time to burn the remains of it and the remains of the people there. The stench blew out over the water; it didn't blow into the land. That was very good, for water purifies stench.

And one by one, entity, in all the sieges and embattlements that we laid forth, my army grew more. And from their beginnings, as it were indeed, I despised tyranny. And I only fought, entity, expecting to die. I did not fight in fear. I never knew that. I only knew hate. And, you know, you pick out the worthiest of enemies, entity, that you would think are greater than you, for they can be your destruction. But, you know, entity, when there is an absence of fear, there

---

7 The hilt of the sword.

is, as it were indeed, a presence of conquering. That is what heroes are made out of, you know.

You know, I wanted to weep, entity, because I knew I had done a dreadful thing and an awful thing, and I carried a terrible sword that was still a mystery to me. I wanted to weep, for this was an awful thing. I had become the awful thing that I hated. And once this scholar had joined me with his bushy eyebrows and his wine and his books, he was bent on educating a barbarian, which I was. I was not a very impressive warrior, you know. I was very small in my body in those days, but I grew later.

As I walked down that which is termed, as it were indeed, a road, that I took off from the road, as it were indeed, and went across to the mountains that I had received my sword, I couldn't get away from the people. I would walk a distance and I would look over my shoulder and they were running behind me. And when I would stop, they would all stop and the dust would fall around them. The old men's cloths that wrapped around their faces and their heads, and it was tied at the side, the wind was blowing it and the dust lay in the folds of their garments. Some were barefooted and some had sandals and some were fortunate to have boots. And they all had baggages with them, you know, their cookery or their weaponry, whatever was their little possessions. And they would line up and they would look at me. And I was a little boy in my sense; not a man, by no means.

And once I ran very fast, and I saw a knoll and I ran over the knoll and I cut straightaway and went off to a small plateau and climbed to the top, only as I was creeping on the ground to look over the edge to see if I had lost them, to watch them looking up at me as I was sneakily peeking down at them. And dogs were barking and asses were honking, horses were whinnying, the dust was furling.

And finally I got up and I looked down at them and I screamed at them, "Why are you following me?" And they just were mute. "I don't want you to follow me. I don't like any of you. You do not belong to me. I hate you. I hate everyone. Do not follow me. Leave me alone." Like a little temper tantrum, you know? And I felt my eyes burning, you know.

And they all looked up at me. Their count at that time was close to that which is termed five hundred. They all looked up at me, old men grinning with no teeth, young women, veiled, hidden behind it — you couldn't even tell if they were women or not — children holding onto their mothers' skirts with big eyes that are illuminating up, mouths agape waiting for something to happen, dogs sniffing in sacks looking for something to eat, banners flying, loincloths. There were all kinds there. And finally I wiped my arm across my eye and I looked down at them and I said to them, "I do not know where I am going. I am just a young man. I am a barbarian. I do not have a soul. I am not to be honored. Do not follow me."

And this one young man came from in the middle of the crowd, and he made his way out. He had a little harp, and he was very good with his fingers. And he was dressed in that which is termed a tunic that was very rough woolen. The dye was very poor; it wasn't even a good dye. It was a brownish, earthish color and it was draped over his body. And his arms were firm and round and they shined on him as if oiled. And the tunic went past his knees and showed very stout legs, like a farmer, and the sun had browned him very good. And his hair, it was very curly and it was very black and it curled around the nape of his neck, and he was almost beautiful. And he began strumming this and singing his wondrous little song.

And everybody whispered and parted and let the young man come through, and he began to sing. And I turned my back and he said, "Great Ram, listen. I have a gift for you." And I turned around and he began to sing, and he sang a song of hope and of the hopeless. He talked about "We are ne'er-do-wells from lands unseen, of families, of ghosts unnamed. We are the outcasts of all that is but have managed to survive when all else have perished. We are ne'er-do-wells of colors and creeds and we are gathered together for our freedom to see. And you, great entity, who have freed us all and fed us, are you our family always to be. And where you are, we will be, and where you sleep, we will lay, and where you thirst, we will drink also, and wherever you go, go we with you."

And the people, the old men, began to sing. Some couldn't remember the words, but they sang. And soon they were all enjoined in a wonderful harmony. And I fell to my knees and I wept. And they sang to the great day of the Ram, the boy conqueror, and they sang and sang and sang. And the women began to dance. And the old women made fires and began to take out their bread and pat it in their hands and put it on the fire. And soon the air was filled with a good stew, unleavened bread, sour wine, sweat, songs, spats from tobacco, animal urine, some dung, and every once in a while a good scent of jasmine. And they made a virtual camp there.

And I went and sat down on the edge, and I did not know what to do with all of this. I could not even take care of my mother. How could I take care of all of this? And the songs, they kept on. I could not sleep. And I would wake up, and they were still singing the same song.

And pretty soon I got up and I heard someone coming up from behind me. It was my old teacher. He has very bushy eyebrows and you can never see where his eyes are looking.

He reminded me of a wizard. And he came up with me and he rolled out the skin and he sat upon it and cushioned himself. He was a man of comfort. And he got out a bottle of his good wine and he drank from it, from his goblet, and gave it to me. I drank it out of the bottle — I was uncultured — and he would frown at me and look away. And he brought me a bit of cheese and a bit of bread and he said, "I have brought someone for you." And I, cursing him. He would not even tolerate what I was saying. And here came the young man with the harp. And he quickly and swiftly moved over there and sat some paces away and turned his face and looked to the stars and began to play. And I was very irritated. And the old man told me to drink up and have some more, and I did. And as I drank, the music got better and better; the sounds got better and better.

And when I awoke in the morning, the sun was already high in the sky, a slanderous thing to do for the sun. And as I looked down on the ground, there was an insect crawling that had crawled over my shoulder and down around my arm, and I quickly put it away. And there was a hand that came out with very good water, gave it to me. It was the one who played the harp, and I refused to talk to him.

And he said, "Lord, permit me. We are all a great family and we love you. Listen to their shouts. They are needing you and they love you. We are coming together for a great coming together. We will go wherever you are to go and we will die with you. Listen to their shouts."

And I opened my ears and I looked down, and here was all of this shouting going on. And the old men were grinning still and the women were grinning and the children were playing. So I asked them to be still, if they could be still, and I began to speak with them. I told them I did not know where I was going but I would go somewhere, and if they did not have a home, they could follow me. And there was a great shout went up.

And everyone was tending to their camps. And I came down and I started across, and as I would stop and look around, they would stop and watch me. I would walk a step and they would walk a step. I would run and they would run. And only when I knew that they were with me, we marched. We laid siege, as it were indeed, to yet that which is termed a castlement not far from that which is termed Onai, and I never saw such warriors. I never knew old men could be so agile when they needed to be. I never learned that women, as it were indeed, could be so swift and could look at the disembodiment of anything and pick it up and put it back together without breaking breath, as it were indeed, without a wincing in their eyes. And I never knew children, as it were indeed, could be so calm.

When that was completed, it had gained even more different peoples, and I had my family. And after each embattlement, when everything was taken care of, they did the same shouting and dancing, the women and their unleavened bread and the men and their spit and gambling. And I had a good family. It went on and on and on and the army got greater and greater. At ascension it was over two million. That is a lot of shouters. That is the story.

I am not a little boy any longer. I am not a barbarian any longer. I am not a conqueror any longer. I am.

Why, say you, I was known as Ram? Because when I was anointed, as it were, upon a great mount I was called the Ram, who comes from the mount into the valleys. I did not besiege kingdoms. I let them besiege themselves. And we brought justice into the land, all the lands. And of the flowers, wherever we trod they grew freely.

Now in my anger and hostility and my desire, as it were indeed, to be noble and honorable to what I felt, I became a great entity, as you would term. Entities, know you what a hero is? Well, indeed I was one. And the hero, as it were indeed, salvages life and puts an undoing to the wrongs of life, not realizing I was creating also a wrong. But I was driven for ten years thereafter to slay tyranny and to make the color of my skin more appealing.

How could I fight a light so great? I fought an attitude. And I ascended, as it were indeed, beloved master, before the last cataclysm of Onai, before the last waters, as it were indeed, were dispensed from the stratum. I had the grand privilege of traveling, as it were indeed, through the Sudan and into Egypt, as it were, and across, as it were indeed, into that which is called the Persian lands — you would not even recognize them anymore — up into Indus, as it were indeed, to the farthest northeastern corner of Indus, to where the sun is especially wonderful. And you know why it sets east and west rather than north and south? What a pity for the sun to have set in the south where it could no longer be seen but for the slim parts of the stratum still covered. Wonderful to be caught up in the east and west kingdoms.

I had the wonderful delight of loving the sun and the moon and the wind and the stars and life, fully, all of my life, in the later part of my years. And what we put under, entity, were tyrants, but to my grave misfortune only to be born again in religious tyrants, which seemingly are deadlier. Are you enlightened?

Run Through by the Sword

There came, as it were indeed, what is termed the tenth year of our march. We came into a valley, as it were indeed, of some renowned fame. The valley, as it were indeed, had always been peaceful with its peoples. And there be, as it were indeed, no tribes, as it were, that maraud and put forth, as it were indeed, tyranny upon the land and fear.

There came, as it were indeed, what is termed a diplomat of sorts that met, as it were indeed, our march outside of the valley of Nicaea. As it were indeed, we had set forth an encampment and had been in our camps, as it were indeed, and settled in in what is called indeed three months nigh in your time. And the women, as it were indeed, were busy with their affairs, and all entities, as it were indeed, that prepare for encampment, master, are continuing, as it were indeed, in sustaining life and caring for flocks and herds, as it were indeed, that follow the entourage, as it is so termed.

There came forth, as it were indeed, in what is called a stormy afternoon, master, with the passing of great thunder and lightning, a runner, as it were indeed, of noble distinction. He came forth, as it were indeed, and brought forth that which is termed a litter of sorts. And all, as it were indeed, the Nubians who brought forth the litter, great in their stature, were wetted, as it were indeed, by the cooling rains and the ominous thunder and had, as it were indeed, still even the hour they approached the encampment, the waters running, as it were indeed, from their ebony bodies unto that which is called the saffron sand.

And they appeared, as it were indeed, to take from their burden and to place on the ground, as it were indeed, and to pull forth the most elegant drape to permit, as it were indeed, a statesman of some notoriety in the land of Nicaea, as it were, to come forth. And the Nubian, as it were indeed, that led that which is termed the front march of this entourage, master, hailed that all should tender themselves for the arrival, as it were indeed, of this entity who had good tidings, as it were indeed, for the march and the hour of the Ram.

I cursed the entity and despised, as it were indeed, his litter and the fact, as it were indeed, that he put forth his pompous being upon softened cushions, as it were indeed, and had gentle and kind men care for him, for in those times, as it were indeed, I would walk with the God of my being but hated and angered all things, for tyranny, as it were indeed, had taken from me the motheren of my being, the sistren of my being, and the beauty of my being. And I am the terrible day of the Ram.

The entity, as it were indeed, was not met by me in my countenance but was seen, as it were indeed, to enter, as it were indeed, what is called my awning. And I made him wait. Soon, as it were indeed, with tedious impatientness, as it were, he voiced, as it were, his impertinence at the unkindness and unfairness that the Ram presented unto him.

The Ram comes forth, as it were indeed, and the entity begins to proclaim, as it were indeed, that the Ram and the host of the Ram had been invited, as it were indeed, into the palace of Nabor in the valley of Nicaea to be, as it were indeed, the guest of a great council that had assembled to compare, as it were indeed, treaties of sorts that the land would not be tormented and burned and perished under by the terrible day of the Ram and his armies.

Now upon this, as it were indeed, I quickened in favor and gave unto him, as it were indeed, my cartouche to return, as it were indeed, unto his noble host, that I would prepare, as it were indeed, a suitable entourage, as it were indeed, and would prepare my times to meet with him in what is called indeed three days in their time. And thus it was.

Upon arriving, as it were indeed, let me give unto you the description of the palace of Nabor. As you approach it, as it were indeed, you cross that which is called a riverbed of sorts that is not alive, as it were, with rushing waters. But the smallest of waters, as it were indeed, trickles, as it were indeed, down stone from stone, as it were indeed, and passes into some forgotten pit, as it were indeed, that issues forth from the other side of a small mountain. And as we approach, as it were indeed, the palace, master, behold, if you stand forth and look to the northeast, as it were, the other side of the river, you will see what is called a "tellamen."[8] It is a great mound.

And there be, as it were indeed, a great fortress standing before us, ominous and awesome and beautiful. The stone, as it were indeed, is of a dull granite. It does not have, as it were indeed, the lightness of beauty and color. It takes on, as it were indeed, whatever the ages have given unto it, all stained in different colors. The gates, as it were indeed, they are bronze. In this time, master, as it were indeed, the black metals, as they are so termed iron in your time, had not been, as it were indeed, finished upon the land as they are now, and all objects, as it were indeed, requiring strength were bronze. The doors were bronze and they were great in their gates. And amongst, as it were indeed, the towers that overlooked the fortress, master, there were great banners. The banners, as it were indeed, were silken beauty in all colors. And trumpets sounded, as

---

8 Archaeology: a "tell" or tumulus is an artificial mound of earth consisting of the accumulated remains and ruins of an ancient settlement. It is common in Egypt and the Middle East to use this word as part of the name of a place.

it were indeed, our sight upon the other side of the small and insignificant river that the entourage, as it were indeed, of the Ram had approached.

Behold, as it were indeed, as we work ourselves up a desolate land, that I see how no things grow and become flourished in it, master. I begin to question, as it were indeed, how this place can sustain in this barren wilderness.

The doors, as it were indeed, of the mighty gates, they do open. And behold, as it were indeed, my company, master, go forward. And we are met, as it were indeed, by what is termed dandies in your time. They are not the lover of women; they are the lover of their own kind. They, as it were indeed, are entrusted by the head of the palace of Nabor and will not forsake him. And they come forth, master, indeed and find us in great favor.

They take us forth quickly, as it were indeed, behind the doors, and there are women, as it were indeed, of foreign beauty as I have never seen that are lightly clothed and heavily decored in what is called indeed brass and bronze and jewels, as it were indeed, and stones, and had found their delight, as it were indeed, in substance.

The gardens, they are wonderful. There is perfumed air, as it were indeed, within the gates of Nabor, and there are fountains that issue forth water that are scented, as it were indeed, with jasmines and lilies and rose flowers. And there are trees, as it were indeed, that are burnished and polished, their trunks, as it were, that when the hand is put upon them they encounter what is called the smoothness of the bark. The leaves, they are green and supple, and the blossoms, they do flourish. It is most peculiar.

And looking upon, as it were indeed, you do not find a simple road, master, but a floor, as it were indeed, that is the whitest what is termed indeed granite marble I have ever seen. It is so white, master, as it were indeed, that I have not seen even snows in highlands compare to it. And it is all clean and pure. We had marvel at this. We put forth our feet upon it and it cools them immediately. There is rest, as it were indeed, and comfort in this refuge in the middle of this wilderness in the valley of Nicaea.

We are taken, as it were indeed, and ushered past, as it were, gardens who loom, as it were indeed, with a procession of fallen flowers outside of the gates of what is called purple and white and rose, and music and soft voices and faint voices of untold stories that go on behind the walls and gardens that lie therein, and women, as it were indeed, of such beauty, master, they tempt all that is in my complement and yet they all seem the same.

We are told, as it were indeed, that our quarters, they are prepared for us. All share, as it were indeed, the same quarters, for we will not be separate. Behold, as it were indeed, there are paintings and friezes that yet within one room after another, master, are greater than the one we have left before. And in the one great room, as it were indeed, that we occupy, it is all an open terrace into a lush and fertile garden. And there is a pool, as it were indeed, with strange fishes. And there are, as it were indeed, cushions and vases and alabaster jars, as it were indeed, and scented unguents, and paintings and friezes on walls, as it were indeed, that depict battles unknown unto my countenance. And there are, as it were indeed, servants that are mute and deaf and know no thing except to serve, that are naked, as it were indeed, save the collar they wear around their necks and who are pleased to serve.

There is, as it were indeed, what is called a small table inlaid with what is called pearl and made of lemonwood, a bounty of what is called wine that is lovely and scented, and what is called fruits and dates and meats and good things they have for us to eat, and immediately, as it were indeed, comfort that we have not known is partaken of. And it is strange to watch, as it were indeed, the deaf and mute entities that wait on us. How know they that we are in desire? They never leave our company and watch all things that we do.

If you go, as it were indeed, from this splendid room unto the colonnaded garden, you will find statues, as it were indeed, and they are not of animals or Gods, as it were, but of peoples who all look the same. They are all beautiful, master. None is different. You will find, as it were indeed, the sweetness and the lushness of the garden and the breezes that are kind upon our countenance.

When the evening, as it were indeed, begins to fall upon the land, lanterns are lit and torches in the garden. And the lights, as it were indeed, placate, as it were, the mystery of this beautiful place and shroud it in mystery and tempt us in desire. There come a'calling, as it were indeed, an esteemed runner to tell us, as it were indeed, that our audience has been prepared. We are refreshed. We are clean. We are given, as it were indeed, a clean linen and kilt to put upon our beings and leave, as it were indeed, and are ushered forth down a long corridor, as it were indeed, and immediately has great and massive vases, as it were indeed, with sprigs of flowers on trees that I had seen in my garden, all alive.

We are entered into, as it were indeed, what is called an anteroom before the great guard. And there awaits, master, a most peculiar mute entity. He is, as it were indeed, small in his character. His hair, as it were indeed, is bleached, that the sun has bleached. His eyes dance, as it were indeed, with a warm fire, and he is muscular, as it were indeed, unto his being and I presume him to be an athlete of sorts, a seeker, as it were indeed, to sports. And he asked for me, master, to the hand, the parting of my sword. It is not given that we should enter this sacred place, as it were indeed, armed. I give the mute my sword, and he takes it, as it were indeed, and looks upon it in the most grand style and considers it a treasure.

And once the doors are opened, as it were indeed, I am permitted to go in, and that of my following is not permitted for reasons, as it were indeed, of what is called preliminary talks, as you so term them in your times, master. I came in, as it were indeed. Behold, I saw men that were anointed and scented and adorned, as it were indeed, in all conceivable spectra of color, what is called gems, and gilded to their very sandals, as it were indeed, in gold. They have surely not known the wilderness and all of its effects. And I despise them, for they rot, as it were indeed, in their own cleanliness. And surely there are sufferers in this palace, as it were indeed, what must be at the hands of their own doing, but none speak, master, but all obey. And they bid me to come in. Their number is four.

As I approach, as it were indeed, I hear the clouded and silken tongues begin to tell me, as it were indeed, how great my army is and how they desire and wish for our encampment to draw close into their valley, master, and into their palace and how, as it were indeed, hopefully their culture, as it were indeed, with our esteemed force can bring together, as it were indeed, an awesome power. And I said no thing. And when one, as it were indeed, be so declarative as to call, as it were indeed, the gathering and the enormous force heathens, master, I had spat upon him and called him a pig.

The entity, as it were indeed, fiery hate flashed forth from the eyes and they moved from me. And there came up, as it were indeed, from my rear guard, master, unattended a most forceful entity, what is called, as it were indeed, a great sword and runs me through.

To feel a blade, as it were indeed, penetrate the back of your being and to break, as it were indeed, the rib, puncturing from the back, and sever, as it were indeed, what is called passages and lungs and the cords, as it were indeed, and cleaves, as it were, the side of what is called the stomach, master, and to find its point bulging, as it were indeed, from what is called the softness of your area of the front of your countenance, master, and to feel, as it were indeed, the hotness of your being exhilarated through the metal that now lies between you, master, is a most unforgettable experience. I had been run through. The entity, as it were indeed, that is so skillful in his wrath with the sword hath put it forth and pushed it further, that the hilt of his sword lie even with my back, and then pulled it out, master.

There is a falling. And I look upon the floor and it come unto me slowly. And as I come unto the floor I can see the discrepancies in the white marble, as it were, that are hued towards the color gray. And as I come unto the floor, as it were indeed, my face strikes, as it were, the cold marble that had no warmth. And as I lay, as it were indeed, unable to see from the right side of my face and unable to speak, for my mouth, as it were indeed, is implanted upon the smooth, cold, relentless surface, there are things, as it were indeed, that call deep within me. And I begin to see, as it were indeed, a scarlet river as it ebbs and flows from my being. There is a crack in what seemingly was a perfect floor, master, and I watch, as it were indeed, as this scarlet ebbs to the floor, master, and drips into the crevice.

It is life — it is life — that flows from me. What of the woman that I loved? She is no longer in life. What of the mother that I loved? She is no longer in life. What of a caress of a sweet woman? I would never know it. And of my children of my seed, have they been bastardized, as it were indeed, and neglected? What of the great tree, as it were indeed, that I hearkened unto at the times, as it were, when hunger ravished my being? And where lies the mount now that once presented itself to me as a home? I will not see it again.

And I hear an echoing, and the sound resounds within my being, master. And there begins, as it were indeed, to appear, as it were, at the back of my throat the hot river of life coming forth, as it were indeed, and it is spattered amongst my mouth. I am dying. I had been, as it were indeed, a ruthless entity that hated tyranny, as it were indeed, and despised despicable men who enslave others. It is the end of my days.

As I watch, as it were indeed, the blood issue forth from my being, master, there is a voice. It speak unto me and it say, "Stand up." It say unto me, "Stand up." I began, as it were indeed, to pull under me the knees of my being and when doing so, as it were indeed, I heard what is termed the empty scabbard of my being strike the floor and scrape against it. And I put forth my palms, as it were indeed, and pulled up my head and raised my countenance, master, that my head, as it were indeed, was erect and even, and pulled up, as it were indeed, my left foot and stabilized it, and put my hands, as it were indeed, upon my knee, not seeing the wound, and standing up. There is a spitting of blood. It is issuing forth from my mouth, master. And the entity that run me through, as it were, dropped his sword and grabbed forth for his amulet that dangled from around his neck, master, and fled. And the men, as it were indeed, with curled beards and anointed heads and skin and countenance, as it were indeed, who first thought me to be immortal, master, have now seen that I am, and they do flee.

And behold, as it were indeed, by gathering all the strength of my being and holding my wound, as it were indeed, as all the river of its blood issues forth through my fingers, as it were, and runs down the legs of my being, master, there comes forth the mute man who be outside of the door who has asked for my sword, and seeing, as it were indeed, the Ram standing forth, begged, as it were indeed, at his feet for mercy. Though he could not speak, as it were indeed, he pleaded, as it were, for mercy. It was given, for how could I, as it were indeed, have possibly the strength to condemn this man who asked for forgiveness when I am gapping through the belly of my being and my entrails, as it were indeed, are beginning to show?

I spoke to this being and asked him to go unto my encampment and seek forth that entity that is called Gustavian Monoculus and the entity called Cathay and bring them to me. The entity went forth himself, as it were indeed, and hearkened unto his being and ran away from me, master, only to return shortly and give to me my sword and left.

If you put forth your fist and grab, as it were indeed, your being where you are wounded and clench it tightly, master, it ceases dying. That is what I did.

Behold there come forth, as it were indeed, Gustavian Monoculus and the entity called Cathay and do things, as it were indeed, to rend the perfect — and to lay bare — the kingdom, and they did so and returned me, as it were indeed, into what is called the legion of women that filed, as it were indeed, the procession of our march. And through women, as it were indeed, master, and their gentle care and their loving kindness did they tender me, master, perfect. Being helpless at the hands, as it were indeed, of a woman, master, who takes charge of your life, a man, as it were indeed, can see life in a different perspective.

I could not forget the voice, master, that made me stand forth, that kept me from dying, and I sought to find the face of the voice. When I was healed, as it were indeed, from that which occurred, master, I began to conquer, as it were indeed, and love that which I conquered. Not all was laid bare, but compromises were met, forgiveness was seen, and the softening of the Ram, as it were indeed, continued great into the march.[9]

I found the voice, master, when I found myself, the God that I was. I was the one who told me to stand up, master. The divine cause, the life, the principle, the understanding, the purpose, was me. With this understanding, master, we changed the thinking of generations to come.

It was not until I was run through with such a great sword was I humbled enough to understand my purpose indeed and why I was penetrated and allowed it to occur. And from the tenth year of my march till sixty-three years in your counting it took me to gain enlightenment.

But I am Ramtha. I desired it. I wanted it. I loved the Unknown God, whatever it was. And in sixty-three years of contemplating and understanding where the hate came from, who created it and why, come I to terms with myself. And when I did, that which is termed, as it were indeed, mind becomes free like a great bird to soar in that which is termed the heavens of thought, wisdom, creation, understanding.

---

9 "Student: I would like for you to tell me of the past life that I had when I knew you."
"Ramtha: I will tell you."
"And who you have been unto me, master, was the mute entity that sent for, as it were indeed, and gave me my sword and brought back, as it were indeed, my complement. When all was laid bare, as it were indeed, in the palace of Nabor in the valley of Nicaea, you were not, master. You were cherished and succored and tendered and became a part, as it were indeed, of my march and saw me ascend. Long did you grow in your years, past that which is called a hundred and twenty. And though you never spoke, as it were indeed, master, for there was no tongue to

Hate, desire to master it: The primitive way was to slay it in others, to slay the reflection of what I despised in others and to do away with it and to give everything to the poor wretched creatures who didn't even possess a soul. Well, even after all of that I could not sleep and slumber in your evenings, for I was a tormented entity, for though had I all things, I had not that which is termed peace, which is the result of that which is termed tender understanding of self, I, Ramtha.

Ramtha's Hovel

On that which is termed what is called the great march, there were periods — Imagine contemplating a tyrant for two years and watching him before you laid siege. In those periods, as it were indeed, they were opportunities to build little cities or to build that which is termed hovels, to house the lot of this magnificent gathering of entities and beasts.

The greatest house, if you would have to put it that way, was — Know you what a plateau is? It is like a mountain someone forgot to finish the top of. Well, in their forgetfulness it makes a very comfortable place to be. There was a great camp and they were beside a river and already the olive trees were already quite large. And, you know, they have silver backs. Did you know that? They are emerald and

speak with, your eyes and your thoughts and your presence of your being, as it were indeed, taught many. That is how you know me."
"Student: Thank you. That's the reason I feel the way I do toward you."
"Ramtha: It is a truth, master. And listen to me at this. Many peoples do not appreciate life or the small voice that speaks to them until they see it ebb from them. Blessed are all peoples who relish life and love it and abound in it and bless themselves for being participants in it. Learn?"
"So be it."
Ramtha's Lifetime, Specialty Tape 021 ed. (Yelm: Ramtha Dialogues, 1984).

silver. They are very beautiful. And I had that which is termed a hovel and I had what you would call a palace where all my children were. That was really their plaything, you know.

But my true home was on that plateau, which I had a clear view of watching the sun work and go all day, oblivious to death, dying, pestilence, poverty, and all of that. Do you know it doesn't really care? Did you ever think of that? Well, and to the night, in contemplating the moon, I always thought that the moon, which I called the Enchantress, that all the stars were her children, that they would grow up and be large moons. They never did. I was in a wondrous place to where I was not cloistered by walls and regulated hallways. I was in a place to where if the Unknown God was somewhere, I knew he had to be lurking out there. And so for there I had moments of contemplation and observation and becoming infinitely aware of the unawareable. Proper term? Indeed. That was, I found, the greatest happiness, you see, because that was the great joy to me. It was simply on a plateau, entity, to where I could be myself and continue with my search.

And when I went to what you would call a palace, there I had all of my children. Do you know what the number one hundred and thirty-three is? One hundred and thirty-three, there were that many children.

Well, it was a good size. It would have fit on the plateau. I would go and watch them, because if you leave siblings alone and observe them and give them all of the things for natural curiosity — for instance, water, a fish, a blooming tree, a thornbush, a bird, a lizard — and you put this all in a garden and make a cave there where they think they can hide, when you really can see them, then you will see a wonderful life unfolding in a beauteous form. And in that understanding of people, they were my form and they exuded the Unknown God with such innocence and virtue and beauty. And so love

I, entity, that if anyone had laid that which is termed a hand to ruffle their hair or even contemplate their molesting, I hacked their head off and threw it into the sea, for left alone they enact God in his purest, most wonderful form.

So what did I feel? Well, I learned there in the palace, as you would term it, great laughter. But when I went to the plateau, there was nothing for me there. Everything went on without me. Nothing even said it missed me when I was gone. So that was the great challenge. Why did it not miss me and why was it there? Didn't it know I was there? You see, it was a combination, as you would say, of those places that made home for me, and that is wherever I found it. You see?

I Had No Teacher but Nature

In having to be taken care of by that which is termed the women in our march, entity, I was bossed, intimidated, humiliated, as it were indeed, undressed before their eyes, and much of my pride, as it were indeed, and hate had to give way to survival, you know. It was contemplating, when I couldn't do anything else, everything around me. I despised man. I would never contemplate man, for he was evil in his soul. Those who possessed a soul were evil in their beings. I was certain of that, yet I was as evil as they were. It is when I contemplated the sound of a nighthawk and the sunrise and how brilliant it is over a valley, and I watched an old woman die one day, entity — the sun, when it was at its zenith — and I realized that that sun had been there when that old woman was born in her hovel, and I wanted to know what the sun possessed that man didn't. And as she lay dying, entity, wildfowl were flying from up the river to the downward river for their evening feeding, oblivious that this woman had died. You notice, have you ever wondered how life goes on when we think it is ending? It is a good thing it does. And I pondered all of these things and all of these things taught me for a long recovery, entity.

When learning about the Source, I did not have a teacher to teach me in regard to the Source or the Father. It was an experience of simplicity that all take for granted, as it were indeed, which is a good and proper term to be used in this society.

I learned, as it were indeed, from the weather. I learned, as it were indeed, from days. I learned from nights, as it were, and I learned, as it were, from tender and insignificant life that seemed to abound in the face of destruction and war. Who was the teacher unto my being was the Source.

In not having the privilege, as it were indeed, of education in that which is called the sciences, not having the privilege to express as a human being, it was I, out of hate, unexplainable hurt, and despair and sorrow that I had no thing else to challenge except perhaps the reasoning that brought me here. I did not know at that time that I was the reasoning that brought myself here, you see. But out of that and learning indeed how to comprehend an element that I found more forceful than man, an element I found much more intelligent than man, an element that I had found that could live in a peaceful coexistence beside and in spite of man, must be the Unknown God, and it was the elements, dear entity, that taught me, you see. And I am very fortunate, for being taught by the elements and reasoning with them I had none to say that I was wrong. And the elements never taught me failure, you see, because they are consistent.

That is how I learned. I learned from something that is consistent, that is never failing, that is easily understood if man puts his mind to it. And because of that, as it were indeed,

I was not at the hands of the hypocrisy of dogma or superstitious belief or multifaceted Gods, as it were indeed, that you are trying to please, or the stigma, as it were indeed, that perhaps we were lower than perfection and could never obtain it. I was never at the hands of that kind of teaching.

That is why it was easier for me to do in my one existence what it has taken many a millennia to do, because they have looked for God in another man's understanding. They have looked for God in governmental rules, in church rules, in history, that they never even question who wrote it and why they wrote it. They have based their beliefs, their understanding, their life, their thought processes on something that life after life after life has proven itself a failure. And yet man, as it were indeed, stumbling in his own altered ego, afraid to admit to himself that perhaps he has erred, continues, as it were indeed, the steadfast hypocrisy that only leads to death.

I was most fortunate, entity. The sun never cursed me. The moon never said I must be this way. The wind teased me and tantalized me. And the frost and the dew and the smell of grass and insects to and fro and the cry of a nighthawk, you know, they are unfailing things. Their science is simple. And the wonderful thing about them I learned, entity, did you know in their steadfastness they utter not one word? The sun did not look down at me and say, "Ramtha, you must worship me in order to know me." And the sun did not look down at me and say, "Ramtha, wake up. It is time to look upon my beauty." It was there when I saw it, you see. That is the beginning. That will never fail you. That will teach you cleaner, clearer truth than anything ever written by man.

There was a great wood up north. I took, as it were indeed, what you would call the meanest of my warriors, entity, the staunchest fighters, as it were indeed — some of them very old and still, as it were indeed, had grit in their teeth — and I took them into a long march that lasted, as it were indeed, eighty-two days in your counting to a woodland up north. And I marched directly into the center of the wood and I found the biggest tree in the wood. You know how big it was? I put an entire legion around it holding their hands like little children and they felt humiliated, and made them circle the tree. You know, the buffoons kept stumbling over the roots and looking up to see if anyone was watching. How great my warriors are, when the roots of the tree can make them fall. I made them hold their hands like little kids. And to hold another's hand, you know, that was despicable. And I walked around them and I laughed at them. I lifted up their kilts and I laughed at them, looked at their legs straining and having their backs to my back, them looking over their shoulder and wondering what the Ram is going to do to them next.

And I said to them, "Do you think this is a great tree?" And they were all in agreement it was a great tree. "What does this tree possess that you do not possess?"

And as they were still occupied with holding one another's hands and not having their hand on their hilt — they were fumbling around and mumbling and eyeballing me and wondering what I was going to do next — they weren't even thinking about the tree. So I went around again and I took out my sword and I put the point to their rears. "What does this tree have that you don't have?" And one by one I jabbed them good, to get the point across.

And then one says, "The tree is taller than we are." That is a good answer. And the other one said, as it were indeed, that they had never seen a tree this way, so it was a new tree to them.

And I said, "But what does this tree know that you don't know?"

And one said, "But, Lord, a tree does not think. It does not have intellect."

And I say to him, "How know you it doesn't?"

"Well, it doesn't get up and move."

"And you think all things that move have intellect? You barbarian, you are a greater buffoon than I was."

Finally I said, "Try to see the top of this tree." And you should have seen them all bringing their heads back straining to see. Now it had become a very serious game to them, for now it was a competitiveness, who could find the right answer the quickest. That is warriors for you, you know. And they were mumbling incoherencies and no one could really see the top, and certainly you couldn't if you stood back a long way. And I came back to them. "This tree does not know how to die. This tree only knows how to live."

And as they were watching me, I turned on my heel and I went and picked up that which is termed, as it were indeed, an acorn from this tree. I said, "See this, this little seed? That is what it looks like. Once it comes from the seed, it only grows."

And they are furrowing their eyebrows now and honestly comprehending what I am trying to say to them. "This tree was here before your grandmotheren's motheren's motheren's motheren's motheren's motheren's motheren was here. It was still a big tree. And it will be here when you die in your own blood. And it will be here generations from now when you will return in your generations as this little seed, for your children will be your future self."

And then one said unto me, "But, Lord, we can take the axes and hew this tree down and burn it."

I said, "Precisely. Only you know that and only you die. The tree doesn't. It only knows to live, to go towards the light. It does not have the thought of destruction in its comprehension, and it is very intelligent."

And they contemplated it, and one said, "Lord, why do we die?"

And I looked upon him and said, "Because we do not know who we are. We, my beloved soldiers, are the bastards on this land for we don't know where we came from and why we are. When we don't know is when we are the waste of this land, we are the death of it. We slay tyranny, but that is what we are in our beings. But we do not know as the tree knows."

And, you know, the man wept. And he sat on his haunches and removed his sword and he wept. He said, "Why know we not, Lord, who we are?"

"Because you have not stayed still long enough to contemplate what is within you as this tree has. And if you ever did, you would never know completely your majesty, for your thoughts change every moment, every moment. But in understanding those thoughts you would be preoccupied at understanding yourself and you would never think yourself into death. You know you are going to die; that is why you die. You even put yourself in a position to war on others to make that perhaps a certainty. You could burn the tree, it is true, but only something in its intellect that knows death could ever do that. The tree will always live. And one day they will make, as it were indeed, a great city here and they will come into this forest and they will lay hew to this great tree, and it will build, as it were indeed, many hovels." And I said, "Do you know the thing about the hovels? They will live beyond the people that build them, and the tree will live on."

I watched all of these things, the truest teacher of all, the elements. The elements will survive when man dies, perpetually.

When I contemplated, as it were indeed, the Father in all his brilliance, there were two main things, as it were, that had me believe in life perpetual: the sun that I called Ra, its advent of glory onto, as it were, the horizons, and its journey all through the heavens, ending up, as it were indeed, upon the western sphere, as it were, and passing into his sleep and permitting, as it were indeed, a wondrous beauty of the moon and her pale light to come dancing across the heavens to illuminate the darkness in mysterious and wonderful modes.

In spite of all of this, I learned this also, that the mute voice of the Father, the sun, though not reckoned with, as it were, controlled subtly, as it were, life. All, as it were indeed, who were brave and gallant or warring with one another and planning debaucheries upon their favor, ceased our debaucheries when the sun went down. And as I saw an old woman pass from this plane clutching heartily, as it were, the crude woven linen that she had made for her son who had perished long ago, I saw her, master, pass in the light of the noonday sun and her life ebb from her body in choking strokes of weeping. And I saw the old woman, as it were indeed, begin to shrivel in the light and her mouth become drawn, as it were, to open to an aghastless expression, and eyes that blazed a gaze at the light undaunted. Nothing moved, save the breeze in her old hair.

And I looked at the woman who gave birth to the son who perished and how great their intelligence was. And I looked up at the sun who never perished. It was the same sun that the old woman saw when she first opened her eyes in her mother's arms through birth, coming through the crack, as it were, in the ceiling. And it was the last thing she saw when she died.

And as we put away the old woman, as it were indeed, I looked again at the sun and I reckoned with it, and I began to ponder it and days and life and creatures that lived in spite of man. And I began to reason that the Gods that are in a man's mind are truly, as it were, the personality of the things that they fear and respect the most, and that the true God was one who permitted this illusion, this ideal, to come and go and still be there when they returned yet again another spring, another life. Quickly I ascertained this, master, that it was to that power, that life, that foreverness that is unceasingly there, where the true reverence of the true God, the Unknown God, lies — life force.

And I began to know who the Unknown God was. He was virtual life, unfailing. I conquered myself through hate, to wanting to destroy myself, an imperfect thing. And I am a virtuous God, lord, virtuous, not that I haven't done anything and that I am pure in my being. I have done it all, and for that, entity, I have gained the wisdom from everything I have ever done and I will never have to do it again. I am virtuous, entity, for I have done all things to become what I am.

How do you know what love is, entity, until you have hated? How do you know what life is until you are at the ebbs of dying? And the sun will set in spite of your death, and the fowl never even look at you, and the ants crawl over your feet, as they are quivering. You don't know that until you have come to the point, as it were indeed, of realization, and each moment brings with it a realization.

There was not a man that ever taught me anything of enlightenment. Enlightenment means knowledge. Knowledge of becomes enlightenment of. It was that out there that taught me.

And, O lord, once after I was able to walk a bit, I saw the wind go through that canyon and up the river and through the grove of olives. Do you know what is on the other side of an olive leaf? Have you ever wondered? When the wind goes through, as it were indeed, a canyon — it hits the river and goes through the orchard — the wind turns the olive leaves over. They are emerald on one side, but do you know what they are on the other side? They are mirthful silver, and you should see the splendor when the wind goes over them and turns the leaf over. They are a most brilliant sight. And I saw it blow, as it were indeed, a maiden's babushka from around her head and let her hair blow in the wind, and she was beautiful. I saw a little girl holding a basket she was gathering, as it were indeed, figs in. The wind blew it out of her hand and the figs went rolling, and it blew up her little skirt, and she went laughing after her figs. It was a game.

When I found out who the Father was and what he was through elevated thought, I did not wish to wither and die, as it were indeed, as the old woman had died or seen many, as it were indeed, the gallant entities of my charge die. There must be a better way to maintain as the sun maintains. Behold, as I am beginning to look upon, as it were indeed, in a state of mending in my direst despair upon my body, once healed from it I sat upon a solitary plateau, as it were indeed, and looked about, as it were indeed, far into yonder where there is a thick haze that slim outlines of ghostly mountains are seen and valleys yet uncharted, and I wondered how I could be a part of the essence that is continuum.

Enlightenment: the Lord of the Wind

But when I sat upon that which is termed my plateau and my armies grew fat, as it were indeed, and much out of shape, there was not much for me to do but to ponder, as it were indeed, as you would call my misspent youth — I was very busy in my youth — and while sitting there contemplated that which is termed the Unknown God and what did he look like and what would it be to be the Unknown God.

Much to my surprise and great relief there came, as it were indeed, a soft wind. And the wind took, as it were indeed, its pleasure upon me that hour. It wrapped itself and furled itself in my hair, as it were indeed, and through my fingers and dried the eyes, as it were, that were tearing, and it caught up my cloak that was long and regal and whisked it over my head. Not a very noble position for a conqueror, you see. But as I uncovered the cloak over my head and put it down and looked around and shuffled myself back into proper study, the wind whirled, as it were indeed, beside me some saffron dust and made it into, as it were indeed, a soft column that went way into the sky. And I looked at the column. And then, as it were indeed, when I was not paying enough attention, it ceased and allowed all the dust to fall upon me.

And then the wind went whistling down into the canyon, down where that which is termed the river flows and by that which is termed, as it were indeed, the wonderful orchards, turning the leaves from emerald to silver. And it blew, as it were indeed, a beautiful maiden's skirt, as it were indeed, up around her waist, with all of the giggling that went on therein. And a child's hat it blew, and the child went racing after it laughing gleefully. The wind, that must be the Unknown God.

So to contemplate being the wind, there was no man that lived that I wanted to be the ideal, no man, for I knew no man, as it were indeed, that I would have traded what I was for, no one. But the wind, alas, performed itself to be very much an ideal. So I called the wind back to me, and it only laughed in its gales in the canyon. And then when I was blue in the face at shouting orders and sat back down upon my haunches, it came and blew in my face softly. That is freedom.

That is when it occurred to me what the invisible power was all about. I contemplated the wind, master, and aligned myself with its elusiveness and lightness and contour that is undefinable. And as I contemplated the wind, it was the wind that I became in my search for becoming.

So, alas, entity, I desired to become the wind and I contemplated on it years and years. Indeed, that became my ideal. That is what I wanted. That is what all my thoughts were bent to becoming. And many times, as it were indeed — and the first occurrence did not occur until six years after, as it were, my resurrection, as it were — but every evening, master, I would go upon, as it were, a solitary place and gaze into the moon and her soft pallor and contemplate the wind.

And then only by accident did I become it, as it were indeed, but when I became it, entity, I only had left my body, as you would call it. The thought was so desirable that it left the body and I caught myself up into the air. And when I looked down upon my embodiment, I caught myself in a fright and felt fear for the first time since I was run through. And it was the fear that brought me back to the body. But I was in that which is called paradise, master, because I thought I had become the wind, as I had been, I am sure, in a place to how the wind would see me if it could. So that is what I did.

I flung myself, master, as it were indeed, unto the ground and beckoned unto the Source, the power, the cause, the wind, and praised it for elevating me through its thoughts.

And I never forgot its grace and its beauty and its bountiful life that I had become that splendid moment and, as I began to reckon as it were indeed, that what gave me that elusiveness was complete, clear, determined thought that was aligned with an ideal, the wind.

Nothing did I want, entity, nothing did I desire, nothing except the one thought of becoming that freedom. And after I did it the first time, no matter how hard I struggled and what sweat broke out upon my body and all of the cursing that followed thereafter, I wouldn't go anywhere. I stayed, and much more heavily than I ever thought I was before, only because I had become aware of how heavy I was, mind you.

And the next eve, as it were indeed, I came unto my place of solitary movement. I contemplated the wind with exuberant joy, and I became nothing. And I went again and again. And I knew and reasoned that the experience was not, as it were indeed, a wishful imagination but it happened. I had seen a different perspective. I had been in the air, as if I was, as it were indeed, a hawk. I had wings that I did not see. And I saw my pitiful self below me.

It was long, as it were indeed, a long time, master, before I became the wind yet again; in reckoning in your time, two years from that event. And this event, master, as it were indeed, happened not on contemplating the wind but going into what is termed a restful sleep. I praised the Source, the sun, life, the saffron dust, the moon, the stars, sweet smells of jasmine. I praised it all. And as I closed my lids, behold, I was in the heavens again as the wind.

It took a long time to reckon that once I was there, how to go other places, and I steadfast myself, as it were indeed, long periods above myself tirelessly. And then it occurred to me, as it were indeed, that which is termed indeed the entity called Cathay was in, as it were indeed, a most perilous position, as it were — for he being a robust character that sought after, as it were indeed, the wondrous ways of women and strong drink and stories, as it were indeed, that were made to be more than they were merely to add the glamour to them — was caught up, as it were indeed, in a perilous position. And I saw life ebbing from him from my viewpoint, master. And in order to, as it were indeed, go unto Cathay to relinquish, as it were indeed, his heel from that which is termed indeed the stirrup that strapped across the horse, the moment my thought was with him I was there in a twinkling of an eye and released the stirrup, as it were, from his heel and stood over him and wished him well. And he thought I was a dream.

But after a point, physician,[10] that thought became slowly the very life force in my whole cellular structure. My soul changed the programming in my cells to increase the vibratory rate within them because the desire was that strong. But it was the peace that allowed it to occur. When you try very hard to be something, you don't do anything but be very hard. You know, that is the effort that is being expelled. But I never lost sight of that ideal nor did I ever forget the moment of feeling when I looked down upon my pitiful embodiment. But it was the peace that went from here, physician, into here,[11] and the controls began to work there. The whole of my glands were changed. That which is termed, as it were indeed, the pituitary began to expand greatly because I had no desire in my loins; it was all here. And that geared up that which is termed the soul to change the vibration rate and the whole frequency in the body, the whole of it, to where I became lighter and lighter and lighter. And

10 Ramtha is speaking to a physician.
11 The brain.

indeed peoples would look upon me and they would say, "Alas, there is a glow about the master" — there was — and the glow and the light was ebbing from the faster rate of speed the body was going at.

And, master, then my thoughts became as one and whatever was thought became. And then I began to lose myself fainter and fainter and fainter by the moon. And one night, entity, I became where the moon was, and there was no more fear, and I was gleeful and mirthful. And that which I did, entity, was unheard of. And yet I came back, but only to anxiously await, entity, to see if I could do it again and again and again. And I did. It became an expectancy, as breathing is to you. But it took that long to program the soul to allow it to occur, you see? Masters, they sit and they think about being this and being that, and then if they are not that in the next second, they give up and they are frustrated. They have no patience, for the thought must transcend itself into emotion and the emotion must carry through the entire physical arrayment. That is how.

I learned to travel, as it were indeed, in moments, that the conclusive God that aligned with the wind and the sun and the heavens is with thought, for wherever thought is, the entity that is God that you are, is — many years. And I knew its passages into kingdoms, into other entities, into lives yet unseen, and visited, as it were indeed, what is called civilizations in the birth of their future. I learned the ways, as it were indeed, of my beloved brethren who would follow me, master, in their advent onto this plane who would discover the Source. You see, when you have come here you do not have memory, for you are caught up in ego, self pertaining to the body now. Once I learned these things, master, I began to teach the Source readily to all of my beloved brethren.

Now by no means should I say that it shall take you, entity, as long as it took me. I was an ignorant man; you are learned. What it takes is accepting it, accepting it: You know it. There is no doubt. You know it. That is what creates the emotion in the soul that brings forth the change in the physical structure, and it occurs.

In finding out who I am, entity, I did first through rejection, denial, into hate, into war, into close death, and a time to be at peace and look around me for answers. I never asked anyone for anything. I never asked my soldiers, entity, their opinions on anything. I only asked me, only me. They could ask themselves if they wanted to join my opinion. But then I was always correct in whatever I did and always responsible in whatever I did. But, master, if you ask a man, "How should I believe, how should I look, what should I believe in, how should I live," look at what they are and what is the consciousness here, as I did in my time. If you do, you will die. That is a truth. Go and ask the wind, "Give me knowledge, wind. Open me up and let me know." And it will do that. It will turn you from olive into silver. And it will go round to holler through the canyon and laugh blatantly free.

I did not trust man; I despised him. But when I learned of the Unknown God and life is when I began to learn of myself and I began to love myself. Then I began to love others.

Ascension

And there came a day, as it were indeed, when it is time that this old man, master, whose days were finished, that all that I had set out to accomplish, being who I was, was accomplished. I made, as it were indeed, my journey across the river termed Indus. And there, as it were indeed, on the side of the mountain called Indus, master, I communed with all my peoples and bade unto them that this truth was a truth, that their divine guidance, as it were indeed, was not through me, as it were, but the Source that had made me, as it had made them. Behold, for their belief, as it were indeed, and to their surprise, master, I elevated myself quite nicely above them. And the women began to scream and become aghast, and men, as it were indeed, who were soldiers dropped their broadswords, as it were indeed, in wonderment. I saluted them farewell, and learn as I have learned, to become as I have become, in their way.

When wanting to be whatever it is that you desire to be, align your thoughts with it. In the wind is a power that can intimidate a solitary soldier and take the earth and whisk it into the heavens in a single blow. And yet it cannot be harnessed or enslaved and it cannot be, as it were indeed, servants to anything, save itself. I contemplated the free movement of the wind and became it. That is how.

The difficulty that all have with this ideal is that they are still caught up in death and old age, and they are caught up in trying to find a machine that will get them there, and they are caught up in complexities rather than the simplicity of the line that the Father is. It is done simply, never arduously.

After I ascended, entity, that is when I knew everything I wanted to know because I went out of the density of flesh and came back into the fluidness of thought, and in that, entity, I was not inhibited by anything. Then I knew the structural makeup of that which is termed man/God. But at that time I did not know. I only knew that I was at peace with what I had done and I was at peace with life. Then I let it flow through me. I was no longer an ignorant barbarian. I was no longer anxious for war, smelling the battle. I was no longer, as it were indeed, anxious and overwrought and overworked. No longer was I, as it were indeed, having thoughts that men have. I was way beyond that. I was into life and into the wonderfulness that I saw in the heavens day after day and night after night. That was my life. That is when the peace came and that is when I became at one with the Unknown God. I no longer fought him.

Now for everyone to be that patient in this lifetime is an arduous task to ask, for they live very fast now and they die very young. They don't know how to live because they live by time. They must do it in a certain perimeter of time or they shall never accomplish it. As long as they feel that way, they shall never accomplish it. They will have only lived by time, and that shall be the accomplishment in this life. Do you understand?

I am the Ram, entity, what they call the God. I was the first God ever known, entity. I was the first man that ever ascended, entity, that had been born of woman and the loin of man upon a plane of consciousness to ascend, as it were indeed, not from any man's teaching but from an innate understanding of life's purpose in everything. My ascension? Thirty-five thousand years ago in your calendar understanding. What is ascension? Taking all that I am into eternity, like the wind. If I had listened to man, entity, I would have perished in that life. Everyone here perishes, for they know they are going to, and everyone here lives for the opinions of everyone else. What a folly.

I learned to love myself when I compared myself to something great and majestic. Whatever man in his being contemplates himself upon, he will become it, for he is the God hidden behind the mask of mankind. The true identity to you, lord, is not your body.[12] You created your body from

12 Lord is another word for master.

that which is termed the loin of your father and the womb of your mother. From that which is termed the clay they gave you, you designed it, but it is not you. What you are, entity, is unseen. No one would ever know you unless you had a mouth to speak and eyes to look and hands to feel. If you were mute and dumb, entity, and catatonic and you lived behind that, they would bury you, for they would never know you because you cannot express, entity, on this plane unless you have a body to express through. The true you is unseen, like the wind. Show me a thought. Show me a thinking. Show me an attitude. Show me a personality.

The great Gods, entity, that made this plane were not of this dimension nor this vibration but of one called light. Your thought's first body is light. Your body is light, but this plane cannot see it for it vibrates lower than light. It is in mass.

The element, the wind, taught me that I realized what I was was not what I am. I am an enigma, even this embodiment, but I exist, and my wonderment is felt by all who come into my audience. Yet who is to say I am real, for what know they of reality, entity, on this plane? Contemplating you beyond the body into the unseen, is an adventure. That is where you will find yourself, not in the eyes of anyone else but in your own understanding. I taught my warriors that.

This day they worship me, entity, as a God in my country. That I despise, for they don't even know what God is. They are a bunch of worshipers instead of "be-ers."

Become you, but know who you are. Look at your thoughts. Look at you. Converse with the wind. Dance in the moonlight. Love the dawn. They will teach you everything there is about life, for they are it and they will live on when all of this dies.

Contemplate what I have told you.

Conquer Yourself

In gaining that which is termed knowingness, you have to humble yourself and look at that which is termed who you are — not what your mirror tells you, but who you are — and see what is within you, the individual, sublime God, and you have to cease holding self as prisoner. The lot of you do it, save one entity in this room, one entity. Know you what a prisoner is? I can manifest for you a dungeon or two that you can understand what truth feels like when it is behind bars and the rats are eating at your feet and the lice are crawling in your hair and the worms are coming from the stench in your dung. You are a prisoner of yourself, as I was, for though the desire to master which come I from was there, I did not know and understand flesh, coagulated thought, and its needs, desires, and its consciousness on a lowered plane of existence. I did not know what it would take. So I ended up in a great conflict at a great and terrible time in your times, all past, in which things had to be rightened in consciousness and within self.

You entities, know you how you imprison your truth? You don't know who you are. I was a filthy Lemurian, soulless. Do you know who you are? Do you know the virtue that lies within you, what you have come here to do? All of your blames for your life you have put and cast at the feet of others, the lot of you have. Everyone is responsible for your unhappiness; that is a great blunder, but also a great learning.

When you know who you are — and in my life it took sixty-three years to learn that — you will look at yourself and see readily, too, who has created all the destinies that you have lived by self-choice and all of the unhappinesses by self-choice and all of the happinesses by self-choice. But it was you and no one else. When you can humble yourself to look at you — look at you — feel you and ask yourself why and then say "I know why" and become reasonable with self, you have taken the bars away from truth, which is the bird that soars in the heaven called happiness, virtue, oneness, and peace.

I slumbered in the latter part of my sixty-three years of enlightenment, slumbered, because I was a peaceful man. I had come to terms with all things. I had made peace with all things and learned to love and respect and admire my greatest adversaries, for I was their threat. I learned to love them because I learned to love indeed that which is termed the elegance called Ramtha, indeed.

Your life after life after life after life, one million years can be lived in one lifetime. Know why it takes you so long and so many lives? Because of that which is termed, as it were, the inability to look at who you are. You judge another, indeed that judgment that you have put forth you will one day decide to live for your better good, to understand others better through the means called self. But for the most part, all of your lives you have learned but one thing in those lives. You have been slow to accelerate knowingness because you have refused to look at who has created it, refused to. Well, I can tell you, entities, that the lot of you, as it were, have lived every conceivable entity that has ever created in that which is termed the genetic loin and womb of woman and man and every color. And you have been, as it were, the least, like a Lemurian, to the most arrogant, like an Atlatian. You have been all of them, all of them. But why not in one life to have, as it were indeed, accelerated what can take in a moment to proclaim and, in the compassion within the soul, to reveal self, looking at who you are.

And I began to understand who was Ramtha. I jolly well loved what I was, indeed, and felt very pleased at the entity so became I. Why? Because I was at peace with the Unknown God who I had found through me, me, and the unique, powerful, wonderful way to create my destiny and to lead my people into greater understanding, indeed. And all that I had done before did not matter when I forgave myself and understood why. Then it no longer tormented me. It no longer hurt. It no longer drove me into conquering.

I have taught you very well. But I say to you — and that which is termed the lot of you still do not know what I am saying — but I tell you that all that you have been you have been for the purpose of gaining understanding, love. Man's creation of right and wrong, of judgmental truths, also created fear and guilt and the inability, as it were, to progress in a spiritual life. When I speak of spiritual, I speak of all life, not just that which is termed something wonderful to speak of in philosophic ways on certain days of your week but always. Then you become inhibited and drowned in your own sorrow and lost in your own scorn and denied by your own self. I tell you, entities, all that you have done in all of your lives, it is all right. God the Father, that is the very vibrance of this wondrous molecular structure, has not judged you. He does not know judgment because he does not know perfection, a complete limitation. He only is. He is the Isness that loves, that is, all himself, and that self is the encompassing power of all of you that are here, all peoples everywhere.

God never judged you, never hailed you to be a saint or a demon. You only did that to yourself, again not knowing who you are. If the Father who in all that he is has found jolly goodness in your wondrous being, and that you have gained and you still have life this next moment to live, to exuberate that which is termed divine self, I assure you, beloved entities, when I tell you you are God, live it, that you can forgive and see and understand why you have been the way you have been, indeed.

So the Unknown God 'twas all things: twilight, the night bird and its rustle in the bush, the wildfowl in their seasonal morning flights, the laughter of children, and the magic of lovers, and the ruby of wine, and the sweetness of honey. It is all things, all things. That is perpetual.

I knew the Unknown God in these understandings. There was no teacher to teach me this. Ram, the master, the conqueror, it was in me to understand. It was the need, as it were indeed, to understand. So I was left in my great wound to heal, to sit, to ponder, to think. All I had was myself, indeed, alone, sitting on a great rock, not in something as wondrous as this. In that I reasoned forgiveness, before there was such a word, and I reasoned self, before there was such identity, and I reasoned God and self as one to solve the mystery.

What I did in my life I have taught you eloquently and manifested boldly for you in your life, that you would have the opportunities to exhibit that same desire to humble yourself to see who you are. And for the lot of you who still close your eyes, I cannot teach that which is termed the only impossibility that ever was, a closed mind. They do not hear, nor do they perceive, for it endangers their cloistered truth of security. You, how know you yourself? Like the dove that is in the prison. Forgive you. The Father has always forgiven you; it is understood.

Look at what you are. Look at it. Look at your anger; why are you angry? Look at your jealousy; why are you jealous? Look at your envy; why are you envious? Look at your insecurities and understand why. Look at your judgments; why do you judge? Look at your unmercy; why aren't you merciful? And look at your laughter; where is it? You contemplate these that I have told you, for sixty-three years you do not have the patience to endure, for you are very rapid. Impatience is scornful. You need it completely now. But in my life, that was my life. And that made me who be I this hour unto you and has preserved that which is termed the personality self called Ramtha the Great, that that which is termed the infinite knowingness of God could come forth through that which is termed this established vessel to teach you in familiar tones.

If you want to be as I am, think like I think. Make it that which is termed applicable to however way and ceremony that you do, but do it.

— *Ramtha*

PART II

FUNDAMENTAL CONCEPTS OF RAMTHA'S TEACHINGS

CHAPTER TWO

Consciousness and Energy
Create the Nature of Reality

Greetings, my beautiful entities and beginners. I salute you. Let's have a drink. You are going to need it. The water represents that which is termed the Source, consciousness everlasting. It is, as it were, an appropriate medium to salute that which is termed God within us all. Well, now let us begin this session with saluting our divinity rather than our fragility.

> O my beloved God,
> somewhere within me,
> come forth this day
> and open my mind,
> open my life,
> that that which I hear
> I may experience.
> O my beloved God,
> of this day
> bless my beingness
> and that which I learn.
> So be it.
> To life.

Beautiful beginners, I am pleased that you are here. Raise your hands, all of you who are here as a beginning group. Beautiful. So be it. Now why did you come here? Are you hoping that your level of acceptance will expand and somehow that will, as it were, change your life? Well, that is a good answer. I like it.

I am that which is termed Ramtha the Enlightened One. I am the entity that said all those words that you have read about, that indeed you have listened to, that you read, and it touched you. It was, as it were, a ringing of truth. Don't be dismayed about the body I am in. Be dismayed at the body you are in.

I unfolded in this consciousness nigh a long time ago in your time. And of that which is termed in this body, this was that which is termed an arrangement, as you would call it, prior to the incarnation of this being. You are here to learn that God doesn't look like anybody but everyone and everything. Moreover, you are here to learn that God in its most exalted quality can be viewed in something as simple as a tree or you.

I Am Greater Than My Body;
I Am an Enlightened Being

I did not come here, unfold here, for the purpose of creating a body that was awe-inspiring, delicious, and beautiful because that has been the idol of worshipers for eons, even today. Beauty has taken on that which is termed physical characteristics — it is no longer spiritual, the inert — and you worship it. But it makes you small because it is a fleeting quality, it is, and it blooms only smally in one's physical life and then it fades. I came, as it were, outrageous, as an enlightened being. And what mean that, an enlightened being? What is your term for enlightenment? It means one who is aware, who has far vision. An enlightened being is one who is pure consciousness manifested in Spirit or mind. And that means that an enlightened being will have a greater quality of the richness of its Spirit than it will in its body. An enlightened entity is one who does not see themselves as their body but as that aspect that is unified with all life. That is an enlightened entity. One who is not is one who views itself as separate, special, different from all other lifeforms. They are the entities that are ignorant.

So I am an enlightened being because in my life and in the times that I knew, I had a grand and wondrous opportunity to be my man-self, to be a human being, to create war, to do away with tyrants. What a lofty goal, eh? But it was not until I betrayed myself that I became humbled, off of my arrogance. And in that humbleness, entities, when I held onto my life by, as you would call it, a gossamer thread, I wondered what was the purpose of my life and my poor, wretched people. And it wasn't until every day that I was grasping for life, and that every day I made a mark that that day I lived through, that I realized that life in and of itself was the prize. And so I sat on a rock and healed myself for seven years, something you would find abhorring. Every day and every night I gladdened my Spirit when I woke up and realized I was here still. And when I watched the moons wax and wane across the heavens at midnight, I was never tired at the scene. I fell desperately and hopelessly, passionately, in desire with nature. It was the moon and the sun that reaffirmed every day that I was alive. I started out worshiping them. I ended up being them.

I am called enlightened because what I learned transcended my physical self. The warrior died. The conqueror passed away. The arrogance, like smoke from a late fire, danced into the night air and disappeared. My ignorance disappeared. So I became a spiritual entity. And what does that mean? That means that I used my brain and my body and my emotional body not for the sake of conquering, achieving goals, and laying waste and resurrection of the Earth. I changed. Instead of becoming the solitude, man to man, force to force, I gathered myself up day after day, little by little, to become a personality that found value not in conquest of this realm but found value in the conquest of ignorance.

What was my most ignorant point? I had many of them, but my most ignorant point was that I hated the Unknown God of my people. You see, my people didn't worship Gods. They knew there was but one God and it was nameless and it was faceless, save that it could be seen in everything that existed and everything that it thought exists. I felt that this God had failed my people miserably and wretchedly. I didn't understand. I thought that if you loved one God that your life would be pleasing, pleasurable, that you could defeat your enemies and live in peace and song and dance all the days of your life. But the Unknown God of my people, which was all life, let them fall into servitude of a much more powerful race, and I hated the God. So I sought out to slay it in every person, because it needed to be conquered because it had conquered my poor, wretched family. That was my most ignorant point of my life, that God could be conquered and that because one loved God, that that kept him safe from harm, enslavement, servitude.

I didn't know that the Unknown God resided in all my peoples and all other peoples and that the nature of itself was that it gave. God is love. What does that mean? It means that God creates and gives and never takes — that is what it means — and that God gave everyone life, this Unknown God, and by giving and supporting that life allowed that lifeform, with the facsimile of its mind, to create its reality. My people prophesied that one day they would fall into servitude. Did not their own prophesy finally become realized because they focused upon it? Of course. The Unknown God is not one mind in everyone; it is pieces of one mind in everyone. And everyone gets to be mindful, however they choose. That is the giving quality of God. No, it did not take a day to understand this; it took the rest of my life because my barbaric nature hated and despised, but my spiritual nature that was small and fragile every day got built. Every day I craved more of it than I did my body.

So then how did I become enlightened? Because being a piece of the Unknown God, I made up my mind that I wanted to be exactly that. And so God, because God loves and we understand that in that, it gives — never takes, only gives — that God within me gave me exactly what I wanted to be: that which is all things, that which can share love with all life.

And know you what, masters? What was the battle I fought every day? Every day of my life I fought my primitive nature that wanted to dispel, doubt. It wanted to move and to conquer. It wanted to cry absurdity. Every day I fought that in myself, for now I have turned to conquer myself, the most arduous battle of all. And what did the conquest give me? At first, nothing, because I could weigh my wounds and I could see all the people and I could recount all of my past victories. I could see that was real, but what I wanted wasn't real, at least tangibly. So every day the real would contradict the unreal. It would make fun of it, as you would say. I would sit there and say, "Ramtha you are a buffoon. You are an old buffoon." Something would hurt when I said that to myself. Something hurt when I said that, so I had to investigate the pain. And when I investigated the pain, something that felt every time I abused it, that became real to me. So for the rest of my life I changed my mind about everything. And I realized that the only reason I stayed in my body was because I had an affiliation with it.

Every time I got angry, I was centered in my body. Every time my body had more power over my will, I was grounded in it. But every day I grew less and less of my body and more and more of my mind.

So at the end of my life, know you how I left this plane? Not in a pine box. I left this plane in the wind. Why should that be my carriage? Because that is the carriage of the Spirit. Why should I not die like natural people? Because I was unnatural. And what made me that way? I conquered my natural self, which was my body, my personality, my genetics, as you would term them. And at the end of my days I had accomplished breaking that gossamer thread to the past.

And so what did I become? I did not become a better man. I became a spiritual being, a God, not a man. And that was what I wanted to be. If the Unknown God was faceless, then it was the power and urges in nature itself. That is what I wanted to be because that most defined God to me, not people, not being a man, but being a being acting upon the knowingness that it is a part of all life. That is what I became.

So why was I called enlightened? I was enlightened because I became my Spirit rather than my body. And so today I am here in this time, as you know it, in another body. And you have come to hear me because you have read my words, you have heard them, you have listened to other people, you have seen a wonderment in your life. And so you come as men and women, children, a Spirit, small, contained within the body. And the job of your Spirit has been every day of your life to keep you alive. That is the only reason you have ever used it. And the only reason you didn't die sooner than coming here is because you used your Spirit to keep you alive, and you have never abused it so much that it has abandoned your body yet. But that is all you have used it for. But it is why you are here, because inasmuch as it cannot be seen but rather felt as a force, it is that which I am.

You didn't come here to see me. That is what you are getting to do right now. And I appear to be that which is termed ordinary, naturally. The teaching then is that God lives in you as what you have defined as a Spirit. But it has just kept you alive. And if you were to see that Spirit, you would never see it looking like your body. Well, I am here in a body that seems contradictory to my terms — it is female and I am male — but it is most wonderful because it is to teach men and women that God is both and neither, and to teach you that what you have been thinking around in that brain of yours isn't necessarily all there is, and also to teach you that what you are, you cannot see.

So most appropriately that I came here to talk to people that I once knew in a time that seems far remote from this time, and yet that time and this time are happening at the same moment. I am here to teach you what I never taught you when I abandoned you. And I am not teaching you to follow me, you can't — not even if you died, you cannot — because only when you die you are only going to get the gift of life that is equal to your ability to accept. And the only thing that you have ever accepted has been your life, no matter how it is. That is what is important to you. Hunger is important to you. Pain is important to you. Being disoriented because you don't like reality, that is important to you. It is important to you to be a woman. It is important to you to be a man. You see, all of these are physical in nature, and hunger can obliterate the Spirit. You can lose your focus on God quicker in the midst of hunger than anything else. So I came to teach you that even if you die, you are not going to be enlightened — you will be a spiritual being but your mind won't be there; your mind will be here — and to teach you what I knew and what I learned.

There isn't one God; all is God. And this isn't the only life you have ever lived. These bodies, they are like garments. You are just wearing this body as this garment in this time-flow. You have worn many of them. So you say, "Why can't I remember?" You can't remember because you are not enlightened. You understand? Your last life you didn't get any further than you have gotten in this one. And if all you were concerned about was that last life, then the only thing that you used was the brain of your personality then, and it was just about the body, as it always is. So if that body died along with that brain, the reason you can't remember — because the body and brain are gone — all you can remember is this life. And you can't even remember most of the days of your life because you have never lived them. You have been absent from them.

Oh, you have lived eons. You are in evolution. God gave you eternal life. What does that mean? That means that when you die, this afternoon, tomorrow morning, that your body is going to perish but you are going to rise in your spiritual body. But the spiritual body again is only as great as the mind that occupies it, which is what you are cultivating now. That is eternal life. And then you will be reborn again if they are still copulating. You will be reborn and you won't remember today. You know why you won't remember today? Because your brain in the future was not here today, but your Spirit was.

So what I came to teach you is not to follow me because that is impossible. And I don't want to be worshiped. I want you to worship you. The greatest temple of God that was ever built was never out of stone and gold and silver and jewels. The greatest temple of God happens to be the human body, and that body is where the Spirit occupies itself in this realm. That is the temple. And if what you learn lifts you inside, then the lifting inside is what is the feeling of the Spirit. If you come here and you are tired or you are hungry or you are bored, that is your body. And your mind is in your body, not in your Spirit. If you are lifted by what you are going to learn, now we are talking to that which cannot be seen inside of you but that which you are inside of you, and it is going to make an enormous amount of sense.

What is going to be the only objection of today and tomorrow? Your monkey-mind, your human brain. You know why? Because if I asked you to explain to your neighbor how broad is the level of your acceptance — Think of those words, how broad, how deep, how high is the level of your acceptance, because that is what belief is. You can never, ever manifest in your life that which you do not accept. You only manifest that which you accept. So how broad is your acceptance? Is it greater than your doubt? What are the limitations of your acceptance? Is that why you are sick? Is that why you are old? Is that why you are unhappy, because the level of your acceptance is unhappiness? That is all you get, you know. You don't get anything greater than that because everything that is greater than that lies in the Spirit. So your Spirit is making you unhappy because you are telling it to.

So the only thing that you are going to have problems with today is your level of acceptance in your carnal mind; that is this up here [neuronet]. And if you are the sort of person that is a victim to your own guilt, if you have done a lot of wretched and awful things and think you are very special because you are so guilty, you are going to have difficulty with what I tell you because I am telling you that you create your reality. And if you are a victim, it is because you made it that way. And you are not going to like that because you want someone else to be responsible for your pain, your limitation, and your lack. Well, I am going to tell you it is your responsibility, and you are not going to like that. The Spirit agrees but the brain doesn't buy it because it can say who hurt it, it can say who disappointed it, it can say why it doubts. It is someone else's fault, never oneself. The arrogance of the human brain, eh? You are not going to like that.

Also you are going to have difficulty with the concept that you are all God, because there are some of you that still like to believe that God is in a piece of real estate called heaven and that he — rather, she — is pulling all the strings. That is why if something goes rotten in your life, you can say it is God's will, God has a gripe about me.

God is a convenient image in heaven, because as long as God sits there he is the one that will punish you for your iniquities: you know, your lack, your lack of love, of caring, when you think bad thoughts you are going to get punished. It is God who is doing that somewhere in heaven. And when you want to be saved, you want somebody to be able to save you. You know why? Because you don't believe you can do it yourself. So God actually works a wonderful part in religion. But what I tell you, that the only piece of real estate called heaven is that which is within you and what you allow yourself to believe, is. And then your God can start right away today forgiving you of your guilt, forgiving you of your lack. Today you can stop being a victim. Today you can stop being sick. Today you can stop believing in the devil and start believing in yourself. Some of you will not like it because you need to have a savior. You are not going to like it because you need to have a moment when God is going to return and get you. This then is going to be contraire to what you believe, because I say to you and what I am going to teach you is about yourself and about what lies in you. There are most of you here that don't believe that you can manifest anything. You have accepted your lack. This is going to be contraire to you. And then the axiom of "believe in yourself and everything is possible," that will come into play.

This School Is about Believing in Yourself

But wait a minute. What is the problem here? Well, I think we have found it. It is called believing in yourself. That is what this school is about, fighting and conquering a self that is only indigenous of this life and being greater than our greatest appetites and learning to accept, where our human brain doesn't, and teaching it to. This school is about resurrecting the Spirit in you, the God in you, to do the miraculous. I am not here to be a savior. I never said I was. I don't want to be. I am here to teach you what I know, which is a lot. And I have the patience of eons to make that happen. I doubt you do.

What you are going to learn is to glorify God in you. And it is going to be a lot of work but in the end, what you are going to become, you are still going to have your body but your level of acceptance is going to be unlimited, indeed. You know why? Because you are going to learn to do miraculous things that will cause you to believe further in yourself.

That is not to say that it is the golden way. It is a treacherous way, because at every step along the way your altered ego, which is the personality of this body, is always there to assassinate you. When you become an enlightened entity it will be because you have conquered your altered ego. And I would say to you then, you who are not clinging to that gossamer thread of life, I would say to you what have you got to lose, a day here, a day there, an hour in focus? What have you got to lose? You know what you have to lose? Only your doubt. What do you have to lose in accepting the miraculous rather than denying it? What have you got to lose? You get up in the morning, I am going to teach you how to blow with the powerful breath of the Spirit and to create your day. I am going to ask you what do you have to lose by accepting that it is true? I tell you, beginners, what you will lose in this life are the limitations of this life as you have once known them to be, and you will gain an eternal life.

Eternal Life? Did I not say that everyone was going to awaken from the deathbed? Indeed I did. But what will be different about you? Because you are going to learn to visit the kingdom of heaven and that dimensional realm while you are alive in this body, thereby expanding your realm of acceptance. And if you pass, and you choose to pass, you are not going to go where everyone else goes. Perhaps you will never have to come back here again. Perhaps you are so lofty that another galaxy with another race of beings that are superbrilliant will be your next parents because you are ready to know what is unfathomable here to know.

Now everyone who comes to this school is always tested, but do you know who tests them? Themselves. The Spirit left alone, fragile, is always given an opportunity for it to develop on its own. But if the person's mind, their altered ego, becomes greater and gets a stronghold into daily life, it will diminish the Spirit. It is very small and fragile. And what happens? Then pretty soon they come back to doubting and lacking and disbelieving, and they start looking for everything outside of them to sort of give them comfort and nourishment because they have lost it inside of them.

And then they come back to school. Imagine having a stampede come back to this august body, a stampede of wild Spirits and hesitant altered egos. Imagine all the cleanup work that has to go on for the first few days. And what is the cleanup work? Even my greatest students in this august body have to be cleaned up. And what does that mean? They have to be told again that they are greater than their body and that what exists in the kingdom of God is greater than their doubt, and they have to be told that. And then they have to be pushed into their disciplines and they have to be made to manifest. And then they go, "Oh, yes, oh, yes, now I remember." Imagine if I have only a week with them, we are talking four days of cleanup work, three days of just getting to another level and learning to accept something they didn't accept before. Three days we have to do that in and then they leave. Do I have students who have changed since they came and sat in your seats? Oh, yes. Do I have students that can do miraculous things? Yes, I do. Do I have students that can't do miraculous things? Yes, I do. Why? Why is there a difference? Why can some and some not? Do you know the answer? How many of you know the answer? Raise your hands, beginners. Come on, higher. Reach for the sky when you raise your hands. Don't stay down there by the armpit. So be it.

Consciousness, Energy, Mind, and the Brain

Now lesson number one: You get exactly what you want. Will you write that down.

I get exactly what I want.

Next sentence I want you to write down is: Consciousness and energy — consciousness and energy — creates reality. Consciousness and energy creates reality.

Consciousness and energy creates reality.

It doesn't matter how you spell consciousness; I do not care. Now the next sentence I want you to write down is: Consciousness and energy and a brain create mind.

Consciousness and energy and a brain create mind.

Now don't go to sleep. How many of you know what consciousness means? Raise your hands. Come on, beginners, consciousness. Don't be afraid. Stick it up there. What if we say something simple like consciousness, it is the fabric of life. That is what it is. I didn't say it was the mind of life; I said it was the fabric of life. And because consciousness is an awareness, then consciousness must already contain energy. What did I say? So consciousness and energy are inextricably combined. They are one and the same. There is no such thing as unconscious energy. Are you still with me? Now consciousness and energy creating the nature of reality would be very simple to explain to your partner. It simply means that reality could not exist without consciousness and energy because reality is, after all, self-aware.

Now the brain. Put your hands up on this sort of melon that you have up on your shoulders, houses the greatest organ ever created. You got it in there? Large, eh? Nice. It holds your face up very nice. The brain is different than consciousness, although consciousness is what gives cells their life. The brain does not create consciousness; it creates thought. Will you write that down. The brain creates thought. That is its job. Now one thought equals mind. Will you put that down. Mind is equated by one thought.

The brain does not create consciousness; it creates thought. One thought equals mind.

Now, beginners, stay awake. Listen to me. You get confused, and why shouldn't you? All of these scholars running around tossing about the words consciousness and mind and the brain, and no one knows how they actually work. But I will tell you how they work. Even though they are only words, they do have a definition. Consciousness and energy is the Source. When it gives life, it gives life because of a thought. The body, the human body, contains a brain, that that brain is the vehicle for streams of consciousness and energy. It is its power source.

The brain's job is to take impulses of consciousness and energy at the neurological level — don't go to sleep — and create thoughts. The brain actually chops up the stream of consciousness into coherent thought-forms that are lodged in the neurosynaptic pathways in the brain. So now the brain can remember a thought. That is its job. So your brain is there to function with a stream of consciousness and energy moving through it, firing the synaptic points, giving you images up here. Mind is not consciousness and energy; it is the product. Mind is a product of consciousness in the brain creating thought-forms or memory. When we take all of those memories and put them together, then you can say, "I like the mind on that person." How many of you understand? Turn to your neighbor and explain to them what I have just taught you. Come on, beginners.

Now, beginners, is there a difference between the terms consciousness and energy and mind? How many of you agree? So be it. Now before we go any further, I want you to understand something. You are learning a philosophy here, not a truth. None of this is the truth. You are learning a philosophy. And what does that mean? It is a teaching. The teaching is about a theoretical concept called reality that we have said so far has everything to do with you, but it is not the truth. Truth is relative. Only what you know as truth is truth. If you don't know anything else, it is not the truth. If someone tells you that there is a twenty-third universe besides this one, they may be telling you from scientific observation. It is their truth, but is it yours? It is not your truth. It is a philosophy, like most things in your life. You know why it is not the truth? Because you haven't experienced the twenty-third universe, and only until you experience the twenty-third universe is it a truth. Now don't be afraid, I beseech you, to learn what I am about to teach you because it does marvelous things. Accept it as a philosophy and that the truth will emerge from the philosophy once you apply it. How many of you understand? So now you are safe. We are not converting anyone.

The Use of Symbols to Express a Concept

Now everyone in antiquity always endeavored to teach what is not seen in symbols. So they always said that God was like the sunshine or the light or Ra and that that was consciousness and energy, and that when we saw the light — you have heard of that term, haven't you? — when we saw the light, then we were what? Enlightened.

Now consciousness and energy in symbolism is like the sun because in its winds it radiates a stream of consciousness, that that stream of consciousness is picked up by the human brain and put forward into thought-forms, which they in turn plant something or see something or create something.

Now this idea of the light, you know, go to the light, that is an archetype in human consciousness — human consciousness — simply because the only way for the human brain to decipher the reality of God and consciousness and energy is to see it as light lighting up the darkness. We understand that in a dark room we can't see anything, but the moment a shaft of light comes into the room or a little flame is lit, then suddenly the light itself, coming at right angles on solid objects, gives a refraction of depth and we begin to see. So the idea of enlightenment came from the concept that ignorance is done away with a light of truth, and they call it consciousness. Now it is not really a light. It is only seen as a light and described as one. When we say then if God is this form here radiating this stream of life to all entities, then that radiating life is God itself being felt in these entities. That is how it has been described.

Now the brain must have a stream of consciousness in order to be called alive. When they hook up those probes to your brain to see if there is anyone home, what they are seeing is the brain's ability to process consciousness and energy, and it is seen by the firing of that which is termed the neurons in the brain, and the neurons fire at different frequencies. So science has learned to determine if anyone is home by the fact that this is firing up here. They call that being alive. If we get a reading, then we assume that this person is alive. But why aren't they awake? Well, because they are in a coma, but they are alive, yes.

Isn't that a remarkable, astounding understanding for you? They are unconscious but they are alive. What is keeping them alive? The Spirit of consciousness and energy. Why aren't they awake? Because they are not processing the thought on a conscious level. What happens when you are conscious? Is when your eyes open and you start processing thought. What is processing thought? The brain taking life, and in different parts — which you are going to learn about the neurology of the brain — is that in different parts it starts to fabricate and fire up the engine. Then thought is being brought forth and suddenly we have a person who is awake and aware, or maybe they only have their eyes closed but they are awake, they are aware, they are present. They are interacting with their environment with thought.

Now the person's ability to think gives them a mind. So how great is your mind? Turn to your neighbor and tell them how great is your mind. How great is your mind? Come on, be honest. How many of you have learned everything there is to learn in this lifetime? Raise your hands. How many of you know it all, all, absolutely all of it? So if consciousness and energy is streaming towards you and through you every day, what keeps you from knowing all that there is, for it is the basis of all there is, your mind. You only know what you know. Now when we talk about you, then we start to separate you from the whole and we start to talk about you as an individual. What makes you an individual? Well, the way you look, the way you talk, the way you think. Well, all of those other things are a result of the way that you think. And your mind may only be the sum total of all the philosophy that you learned in school. You can say, "Well, now I graduated from school."

"What does that mean?"

"That means that I remembered everything they taught

me and I passed all the tests on their memory."

"But did you experience it?"

"No."

So then your brain is full of theoretical philosophy that you have agreed must be the truth, but it isn't. The person who taught you that, that is not even their truth; the person who discovered it, it is truth. How many of you understand? So what is in your head? What is in your head is everything your parents taught you, everything that your schools taught you, everything your history taught you, everything your culture taught you. But how much of it is the truth? In other words, is anyone home or is this just a recording?

You know why no one creates miracles any longer except in the field of technology? Because everyone has assumed that everything they have learned in their head is the truth. Miracles only come at the expense of expectancy. Does that make sense to you? In other words, it is what you didn't learn. It is what you don't know as truth, that you expect it to happen, and it does. That is truth. So your mind is filled with so much gibberish. And how much superstition do you have inside of you? Do you walk under ladders? Do you believe white is good and black is bad? Shame on you. Do you feel guilty? Shame on you. Do you still feel guilty? Shame upon you. Now here is the point. The point is that one of the reasons you are so bored with life is because you can only do what you know is the truth, you know, that happens every Saturday night, that happens every Sunday morning, that happens at work. You are bored with your job and you are bored with your life. Do you know why? Because you keep doing the only thing that you know how to do and that is the only truth that you have. Everything else is conjecture. So how great is your mind? It is only as great as your truth. Will you turn to your neighbor and repeat that, kindly, how great is your mind.

The Voice of Our Spirit

Now, beginners, am I overloading you? Oh, I only have two days with you. And when am I going to see you again in this form, and when are you going to be ready to learn? Perhaps not ever again, or perhaps you will come back and you will continue to learn. So what do I need to do with these two days? I need to tell you as much as I can put into verbiage and make you explain to your neighbor, who you are awfully shy about talking to neighbors, make your brain work, make you talk, make you think so you can create a little miracle here in these two days, so I send you back in the world with a whole lot of hope and a whole lot of desire to know truth rather than philosophy. And then perhaps when you come back to me you will be running here like the rest of the mob.

Now what is the purpose then? What is the purpose? Imagine what your Spirit is thinking. Have you ever imagined your Spirit Saturday night? "Give it up. Are we doing this again today?" Imagine your Spirit, you know, your God. "What is wrong with you? Can't you do anything else? Can't you think on your own? Can't you shut up long enough to let me talk to you? You have bad breath." Imagine what your Spirit is talking to you. "I don't want to go to work today. I don't want to do the same old thing today. Do you know why I don't want it? Because it is me that you use to do the same old thing every day. And I am getting smaller and smaller and smaller. And if you are starting to look like a prune, it is because you have used me up."

Imagine your Spirit when you are going to be spiteful to someone, because it empowers you to be spiteful to someone. I know what this feels like. Imagine your Spirit sitting back in horror as your monkey-mind proceeds to attack viciously and, like a puppet, it is being used to slug it out with some innocent person. Imagine your Spirit sitting there going, "Will you shut up. Why must you be this way? We do not want to make war. We want to make love. Love this person." Imagine that voice. Imagine that voice in your head at the moment of your greatest tempest. And you are angry, and it says to you, "Calm down. Let's love. This is us that we are attacking." Imagine that voice. You don't want to hear that voice. You tell it to shut up and you get even madder and you punch even wilder. Imagine your Spirit. What else is it supposed to do? You know, the reason you are growing old and you are getting an awful lot of diseases is that it has had it with you because you are supposed to grow. That is why you are here. What does growing mean? It doesn't mean that your body needs to grow. It means your wisdom needs to grow. Your Spirit is the life force that you use up in one lifetime. It is large when you are a child; it is all over the place. And as you start spilling your seed and having your season of blood and as you start forming opinions about the world, it starts to get smaller and smaller and smaller because you are using your Spirit up to create with.

Now you know why you are dying? It is because you have used up a vital energy source about eternity in the forms of created thoughts. And one of these days that Spirit is not going to wait to get rid of you. It is going to shake, shake, shake, shake until you fall off. How could a Spirit be so ungodly? That is just the point; it is. You are here to grow, my beloved people. You are here to create reality, not to continue status quo. You are here to grow in knowledge, philosophy, and then in truth. You are here to live, not be afraid of life. You are here to use your brain to create thoughts and to conquer your ignorance.

What happens when a person becomes enlightened? They conquer their ignorance. What does that mean? That means that they develop their Spirit rather than their altered ego, their personality, their body, and they work every day in embodiment of that energy. So what happens to them? They don't ever really grow old. They have dynamic energy. They can create. And their level of acceptance is extraordinary. If you ask them do you believe in this, they will always say yes. They will never say no. They will say, "I have experienced that already. I have owned that." What does that mean? "That means I created it as a philosophy, I manifested it as an experience, I experienced it and, boy, was I in trouble. But after the experience, I know about it. I have wisdom. I have truth." How many of you understand?

Now that doesn't mean that you have to be a goody-two-shoe or three-shoe, whatever you want. It doesn't mean that. New Age is not new age; it is forever age. What it means is being greater than your body and being greater than your prejudice, being greater than your lack. And that is not having a positive mental attitude, because if a person has a positive mental attitude, it simply means that they really have a negative mental attitude in which they are trying desperately to have a positive mental attitude, so we have a veneer of possibility positive. I want you to change and to be it.

The Discipline of Consciousness & Energy^{SM}

Consciousness and energy creates the nature of reality. That reality created the human body and with it its greatest organ, the human brain. The brain does not create consciousness and energy. It is an instrument of it, a machine. Its job is to take consciousness and energy and to freeze-frame it into memorized, biochemical thought, that that thought then can be added onto to create reality, and that whatever sits up here as a thought is created out here in the time-flow. And the idea is to take consciousness and energy, the virgin, and create thought that is evolutionary, and to be greater and to think greater so that that in turn creates your life greater. So then God, the Spirit, is now evolving in you. And what is happening within you will happen outside of you.

I am going to show you the discipline of Consciousness & Energy[SM]. The discipline means this, that one of the first things that you learn in this school is how to still the mind and to find a place called the Void — the Void is the Mother/Father Principle; it is where consciousness and energy springs from — and how by moving energy from this center to this center, in other words, moving energy from the base of your spine to the midbrain between that which is termed your neocortices, that energy is given to the brain so the brain is cleaned out and all it is is just idling, so that then who you are disappears, what you feel disappears, what you are worried about disappears. All other things are wiped clean in the brain because if the brain is the mechanism for creating tangible reality via thoughts, then we have to clean it up and get it pure so that whatever we place here [frontal lobe] as a focused, conscious thought will manifest out here [our environment] in absolute clarity.

So before I give you a break and give you an opportunity to change your mind about being here, I am going to show you with some students what it looks like.[1]

---

1 See *Chapter Eight: Closing Words,* pp. 265-269. Students who wish to learn and practice Ramtha's discipline of C&E® must attend a class through Ramtha's School of Enlightenment and receive instruction personally.

And it is shocking, to say the least, it is frightening, and you may even be embarrassed. It also shows you your level of acceptance, which you need to learn about yourself. What don't you accept? What are you prejudiced against? What do you not believe in? After you have watched these students do this discipline and every one of the students around you do that discipline, I want you then to make up your mind if this is what you want to do, if you want to spend the rest of the day here and surely be counted tomorrow, because when we break, you will have an opportunity to go and get your gold back and then I want you to leave. But I want you to leave having at least an open thought that surely something wonderful must come out of this mess. And when you are ready, come back and see me. Of course you will be older and wiser then.

Remember, the work is about you and it is about developing that aspect of yourself. We have students in this school — and not just one, but many — who have brought dead creatures back to life. We have many who have created miraculous healings in their life. They are so documented. Every student in this school has created reality for themselves. They have changed their lives to various degrees. They have developed what you call psychic power. That is only a phenomenon of that which is termed embraced in the entire godhead.

When you come back we are going to go to work and we are going to talk about the origins of self, how you got into this pickle, what is the reason for you being here, and how to get out of it. And tomorrow you are going to learn the discipline of Consciousness & Energy[SM] and how to create three things in your life that you wish to have happen and how to change three things in your life you would like to get rid of. I love you. You are excused. So be it.

CHAPTER THREE
Origins of the Self

I salute the God within you. Pray let us never forget where it resides. And let's have a drink.

O my beloved God,
I call forth
that which I learn
this day.
I expect
to experience it.
God bless my life.
So be it.
To life.

Importance of Articulating the Teachings

Now from here on out you are going to learn a lot of philosophy. But in learning this philosophy I want you to transfer it from that which I am to that which you are, so this is what I require for you to do today. Pay attention, listen, concentrate on what is being said because I am going to break frequently and I am going to ask you to turn to your neighbor, your innocent neighbor, and tell them exactly what you learned.[1] I want you to put it in your words. When

1 This is an important characteristic of Ramtha's teaching technique that helps to pause, contemplate, and articulate in your own words and understanding the information discussed up to that point. It helps in staying focused on the subject and retaining the information. We suggest to the reader to follow Ramtha's instructions, regardless of whether you have a partner or not.

you learn to open your mouth and transfer what you hear into verbiage, it starts to stay inside of your brain. And in particular if indeed you can bring it forth and put it in your own words, now instead of a teaching from me it is a teaching of you. How many of you understand?

Now mind creates reality. Every day of your life has been that which is termed a product of the way that you have thought. If we can understand this process and expand that which is termed your level of acceptance and indeed your level of understanding, you should, according to the philosophy, experience truth by manifesting it in your own life. So I want you to be able to speak today everything that I have taught you, to be able to draw it out, to be able to use your hands, simple as a child, and to be able to express what it is that I am teaching you, that you may express it to someone else. Think of that which is termed your partner as a confessor, or think of them, as it were, as if they are yourself and talk to yourself in a way that you want yourself to understand. Don't sit there, I ask you, and be quiet and deaf. Participate in everything I ask you to do. If you do, you will be enriched at the end of the day.

You are little children. There are civilizations and entities on other planets, in other galaxies, in other dimensions, in other time-flows that are much more advanced than you are. However, having said that, there are other entities on a few other worlds that are a little behind you, but not much. You are little children. You are, as it were, part of a community called God. And what we have referred to you for eons is a term that is most befitting to the human drama, and that is the term forgotten Gods. You forgot about your divinity and got wrapped up in your physicality, your material self.

The Void, the Source of Everything That Exists

Now let us go back to the beginning, you know, the beginning that happened only a moment ago. How did this all begin? The teaching that I am going to give you today may be filled with that which is termed verbiage contradiction. However, there is a level of understanding that transcends words, so words become that which is termed a cripple's tool in order to explain that desire that cannot be expressed. We are going to be talking today about how all of this, the vastness of space and time, all came about and where did you come from, why are you here, and what are you doing not getting to where you should be going.

Now take out a piece of paper, clear, clean paper. Let it look like this, with no thing upon its surface. We are going to talk about an enigma in terms of two-dimensional expression. I want you to repeat this word, the Void. Again. Now the Void, let us determine what the definition of this word should be. The Void is vast, and yet in its vastness there is nothing. So it is one vast no-thing. No-thing means elemental, even thought. There is nothing, no-thing. So it is a vast nothingness, empty. And yet in the face of and in the space of nothingness exist and coexist potentials. And so we would say that the Void, although it is a vast no-thing, it is potentially everything. So I want you to repeat this: One vast nothing materially — say it — all things potentially. Turn to your neighbor and define the Void. One vast nothing materially, all things potentially, that is the Void.

The Void, to that which is termed a finite mind, is difficult to conceive. So perhaps the most graduated visual that can be utilized is to think of space and all of the stars and planets and gaseous clouds and nebulae that exist therein and see it as far as you can see, and then in the next moment extinguish all of the light from space. Now we have a close mental concept of the Void, one vast nothing. Now how old is one vast nothing? It is timeless because time is a potential that will spring from it. How many of you understand? So the Void has always been. Now do you experience the Void in your normal life? If any of you have ever allowed your mind to rest or take a pause naturally and you are staring with your eyes transfixed, and in that moment that you are staring and transfixed you are not thinking of anything, you are empty, that is experiencing the Void. Now the Void in its alwaysness is called the Mother/Father Principle or it is called the Source, the Source in which all life springs from. But how does life spring from a no-concept? How does the Void give life to that which it is not?

So this is what happened. One morning at 10:30, Tuesday, I believe,[2] the Void did a spectacular thing — a thing.

FIG. 1: THE VOID CONTEMPLATING ITSELF

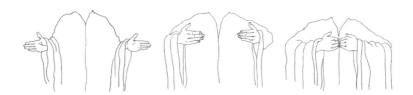

The thing was it contemplated itself, contemplated itself. Now I want you to spread your arms out like little children. Contemplation as a visual is seen in this way.

---

2 This phrase is intended as a humorous figure of speech and not as a factual piece of information.

Where the left and the right come together is the center of the magnet. Where the negative and positive come together is the center of the magnet. In the magnet's center it is neither negative nor positive. It just is. So now the Void — spread your arms out — the Void, being one vast nothing, contemplated itself and the moment that it did, a moment was born.

FIG. 2: POINT ZERO

Now I want you to take your blank piece of paper and I want you to turn it and fold it in on itself. And where it meets I want you to take that which is termed a writing instrument and put a little black mark up there. Just turn it in on itself, and wherever both ends of the paper meet, put a little mark. That is to give you a mental picture of how all of this began.

FIG. 3: PRACTICAL EXAMPLE OF THE VOID CONTEMPLATING ITSELF

Now remember this is simple, elementary. The Void contemplating itself created an echo of itself. In other words, it created an alteredness of itself and we recognize that in this dot. This is the first time a potential is born out of the Void that always was. And that potential, where it contemplated itself, becomes the echo but concentrated. It is an evolution. Now this is what you began as, this here, and this entity here is contained as consciousness and energy.[3] This is consciousness and energy. Now in this was your beginning and yet still you have not begun. You have only been contemplated upon by the Void. All of this is the Void and we are seeing it in that which is termed two-dimensional, linear time.[4] But this spot here now becomes a reference point. This then is called God. So I want you to write beside this "God I am" straightaway. This contemplation point is consciousness and energy beginning. This [the Void] is the Mother/Father Principle that gave it life and this is where you started.

Now the Void talks to this little entity and it says, "Good afternoon. I have longed for your presence in my midst. I am delighted with your countenance. I want you to make of me whatever you want to do. I am no longer alone. You are now with me. Go and make of me whatever you please."

---

3 See Fig. 2: Point Zero.
4 See Fig. 3: Practical Example of the Void Contemplating Itself.

Now when your mother and father told you that when you were wee little entities, you got into trouble. So you ran around the house and you ran around outside and you did all the things you wanted to do, and then you came in and only found out that that wasn't exactly what they had in mind. How many of you remember that? The only difference is with this parent there were no constrictions; there was a permission to grow and to expand. So now imagine what you would think, "Go and make of me whatever you want to do." Now understand there is no time in this Void, and if there is no time, there is no distance, and if there is no distance, there is no space.

So here is what you start thinking. You think, "All right, I will run over here, over here. This looks fun." So the moment you appear over here you are back here, because "here" is "there" in the Void.[5] How many of you understand? There is no time, so over here doesn't exist. This becomes this place here. So then you get a little frustrated and you say, "Well, that is all right; then I will go down here." But what is "down" to the Void? So you end up down here and you say, "Aha." But the moment you perceive that you are down, you are really back where you started because in the Void there is no time, so everywhere is the same. How many of you understand? This entity was all over the Void but never went anywhere. And we can only anticipate from this point of reflection how many eons that entity must have stayed there trying to be all that its parent had said for it to be, because "all" was certainly up for a new understanding. Everywhere this consciousness threw itself, it already was, so it never went anywhere.

---

5 In other words, since there is no point of reference to measure time and space, every instance Point Zero tried to move, it found that it ended up in the exact same place where it started. Point Zero could not perceive any change or movement since it did not have any point of reference to measure it against.

FIG. 4: POINT ZERO ATTEMPTING TO MOVE IN THE VOID

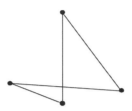

And so one day, Friday, as it was sitting there, it contemplated itself. Show me what it did. Come on, contemplated itself. Beautiful. Every time you contemplate yourself, you evolve. So it turned all of itself in on itself and as soon as it did that, the point of contemplation was created, sort of like this. Take both of your hands and hold them up in the prayer position, slightly to your left to give you some breadth.[6] Now this is that little point turned in on itself. The moment it turned in on itself, do you see how it became divided? How many of you see? And the moment it did that and came back, it was two instead of one.[7]

FIG. 5: CREATION OF THE MIRROR CONSCIOUSNESS

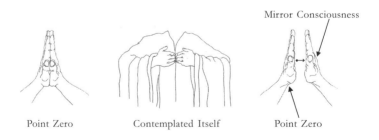

Point Zero   Contemplated Itself   Point Zero

6 See Fig. 2: Point Zero.
7 See Fig. 5: Creation of the Mirror Consciousness.

Creation of the Mirror Consciousness and Time

Well, now consciousness and energy has company, has someone else here. So the Void that gave birth to it, it in turn gave birth to this [mirror consciousness]. What is this? This is yet a lower aspect of this [Point Zero]. Now don't go to sleep. Hold your hands up. This space here is very unique in the Void because for the first time we have two points of consciousness — one, two[8] — and yet between those two points we also have a new reality, and the reality is called time. And why is time existent only here? Because we have a distance between two points of reality. Close them up. If you close up this hand, is there any time? Is there any time? (Audience: No.) Is there time now?[9] (Audience: Yes.) How many of you agree? You do? Wonderful. Well, now we have the second great creation: We have time, distance, and space that is offset by another consciousness.

FIG. 6: ILLUSTRATION OF TIME, USING THE HANDS

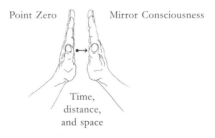

Point Zero   Mirror Consciousness

Time, distance, and space

---

8 See Fig. 6: Illustration of Time, Using the Hands.
9 Hands spread open.

So how many of you have heard of the seventh level of heaven? This is the seventh level of heaven. This is where we began. Now close them back up, now we are one. Separate them, we are two. How fast is the reality on the seventh plane of heaven? Well, let me ask you, if you had the consciousness back as a seventh-level entity and if you had a thought, how long would it take for it to manifest?[10] That is all.

Now we have creation, right here. This is the God and this is the mirror consciousness of God, right here. So now we have life happening. Between these two hands exists a whole reality just like this Earth plane, except it is the first plane, the seventh plane. And after you lived here, for how many eons we dare not guess, what did you do when you got ready to go further? Turned in upon yourself; correct? But now we have a little problem because the self has got something wandering out here. It has got this other hand. So this [Point Zero] needs to get this [mirror consciousness], the message, to do the same. So what it does is they collapse time. Now they are one, are they not? And when they contemplate, they are not contemplating the seventh heaven any longer. They are contemplating the next heaven because they have already lived the seventh heaven. They contemplate, pull up, here is the seventh heaven, but the program is to go out here. Now we are in the sixth reality.[11] What is different about this heaven than this heaven? Will you show me? Excellent. Is the time slower or faster in the sixth heaven? Slower.

---

10 Thoughts manifest instantaneously on the seventh plane.
11 See Fig. 7: Sixth Level.

FIG. 7: SIXTH LEVEL

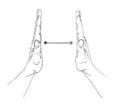

So now if you lived in the sixth reality, how fast would it take from the point that you conceived the thought to reality happening? Now would you say you are a little slower than the person who lived in the seventh reality? Yes. That is the difference.

Now we have a wonderful thing happening here. We have levels. Here we have the seventh, and now we have the sixth. Notice that the distance between these two is longer than the distance between these two. How many of you see that? Well, that is the secret of time that we are going to talk about. It happens to be the relationship in consciousness, not perennial points, coagulated points like, for example, a distant star. It is consciousness. So now we have true creation going on. We have the Void and from the Void, inside of the Void, we have consciousness and energy that has learned the secret: Turn in upon yourself and contemplate. When you do, you become expanded. So now we have a ladder being built, and we have this mirror consciousness here always reflecting to the God consciousness here.[12] And what exists between the two are called potentials of life. So the seventh heaven had a different reality than the sixth heaven. How many of you agree?

12 See Fig. 6: Illustration of Time, Using the Hands.

FIG. 8: FIFTH LEVEL

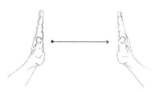

Now, students, I want you to now re-create the picture. I want you to draw Point Zero like you have done. This is your godhead. I want you to drop down and draw another point. Between these two points is the seventh plane. Close up this, come down here, create another, sixth and seventh. I would like for you to do that all the way down until you have seven dots.[13] Participate. Just do this on your Void paper. Now with your hands, put them up and start up here and in front of yourself gauge each one of these levels. Come on. Now what level are we on? Is the time on this level [fifth level] slower or faster than this level [sixth level]? (Audience: Slower.) How many of you agree? So be it.

Now the triad is one of the most holy forms that was ever created in sacred geometry because the triad, as it were indeed, maps that which is termed creation's thoughts, from which the essential point of creation everything springs from. Triangles, like we are going to draw here, is the principal element in life as consciousness and energy on this plane. So what we are going to do here, if this then has got a shorter time [fifth level], we are going to determine that by placing that which is called a horizontal line, approximately this long.[14] Would you draw a line like this. This is slower time

13 See Fig. 9: Descent of Consciousness and Energy from Point Zero.
14 The horizontal baseline at the fifth level of the triad.

than this, so we draw a longer line. And every line that we draw, we make it a little longer than the one that preceded it. Have you all drawn this?

FIG. 9: DESCENT OF CONSCIOUSNESS AND ENERGY FROM POINT ZERO

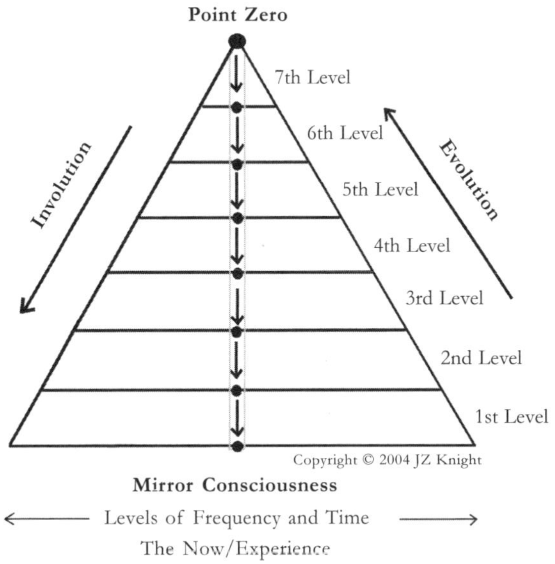

Point Zero

7th Level

6th Level

5th Level

4th Level

3rd Level

2nd Level

1st Level

Involution

Evolution

Copyright © 2004 JZ Knight

Mirror Consciousness

←——— Levels of Frequency and Time ———→

The Now/Experience

Now this looks very simple to you but these are timelines. This is a timeline based upon this plane. Today you are all down here [first level]. You are living in this slow time and on this timeline. In the same room, in this same room, we have another level of consciousness existing in another timeline in the same space you are occupying, except their time is faster than this time. In another, same place you are sitting, we have even a different timeline. Its frequency is even more rapid, on and on and on. So where you are sitting is being occupied simultaneously in dimensions by other lifeforms. And the reason that you can't see them is because

they are vibrating or their energy frequency is much more rapid than the one that you are occupying now. And as far as Earth magnetics at eight hertz, you are vibrating at eight hertz, but a spiritual entity sitting in your midst may be vibrating at three hundred and twenty hertz. How many of you understand?

Now when you were born, up here, Point Zero, right here, when your God created you right here and you began the journey through contemplation coming down, you were growing deeper and deeper and deeper in the Void.[15] You were also creating a great linear time from this to this [two points of consciousness]. This [Point Zero] never moves. Only this is mobile, this consciousness here [mirror consciousness]. When we were in descent, all of us, we called that the Book of Involution. So I want you to draw a line down this side of the pyramid going down, and I want you to write in your language the word involution, involution. Show it to your neighbor when you are finished.

So now how did you get down here? Well, whoever said that this was a bad place? Nobody made you come except yourself. You are the one who wanted to be here. You are the one that made the fall. You are the one that picked up this body and picked up this timeline and for eons you have reincarnated into various bodies in order to follow the destiny of this timeline through your own exploration.

Now I want to ask you something. You are sitting here vibrating. Look at your hand. Does your hand look the same as your neighbor's hand? Are they as dense as each other's? Well, that means that both of your hands are vibrating at the same rate of speed; otherwise you couldn't see them if they weren't. So everyone here is the same. Everyone's

---

15 See Fig. 9: Descent of Consciousness and Energy from Point Zero.

frequency in the body here is the same. That body's frequency is tied into this here. Now let me ask you, just because you are here and you can't see this, does that mean it doesn't exist? How many of you agree? Everything is happening under the shadow of this point, and it is all happening within the time and the space that you are sitting in right now. This is an illusion, this timeline. This line, right up the center of the pyramid, is called the Now. Where you are sitting, there is an extraordinary level of intelligence sitting with you. That level of intelligence you can't see because it is vibrating at a greater rate of speed.

Now we are going to do a little demonstration here. Take a colored pencil. And if we know that this is the length of time, if this is consciousness, then it must be energy that is flowing between the two [points of consciousness]. I want you to do this, will you. Energy undulates just like this [a wave]. This undulation or bell of energy is the oscillation time that it takes from this point to this point. So this is an energy line. I want you to draw those energy lines just like this on the seventh level.[16] Will you do that.

FIG. 10: ENERGY OF THE SEVENTH PLANE

Now when both of your levels of consciousness are right here, then all that exists is what is between the two of them here and here. Now when we close this back up,[17] where

---

16 See Fig. 10: Energy of the Seventh Plane.
17 See Fig. 2: Point Zero.

does energy go? Come on, beginners. If there is energy dancing between these two levels of consciousness, when we collapse them where does the energy go? It is collapsed back into consciousness. Now when we pull this hand out to the sixth level, what happens to that shortwave consciousness that used to exist from here to here [seventh level]? When we pull it out to here [sixth level], what happens to that level of energy? Does it still exist? It still exists. But now if this and this [two points of consciousness] are sitting in what we call the sixth kingdom, what has happened to the divine energy of the seventh? It is winding down. It has curled in upon itself, like this. And in the meantime we have this longer wave of energy and a slower time ratio in consciousness creating reality. So if you are living here, and you used to live there [seventh plane] but now you are living here [sixth plane], does that mean this [seventh plane] no longer exists? (Audience: No.) How many of you agree? So be it.

Now what I want you to do, I want you to fill out this pyramid. And the reason I want you to do this — it is very simple physics — we are going to learn about time, vibrational mass, energy, and why you are here, and why you can't see the other planes. I want you to realize that they all exist, but it is a matter of where you have been focusing your energy at is where we are going to find you. And what is going to happen to seventh-plane energy? We have it wound up here [sixth plane]. What is going to happen to it when we move it down to the fifth plane? Is it going to get tighter? Are we pulling it and making it get tighter? How many of you agree? It is a truth. So then it becomes the dots. What happens to sixth-plane energy? Come on, come on, beginners, wake up. If energy is being wound and tightened down, if we are taking this energy and pulling it to the fifth level down here but it is only vacillating at this wave frequency from here to here, if we pull it down here, is it going to spring? It is, and it is going to spring around the seventh energy that has already started the nucleus.

So what I want you to do with your little workboard, consulting your neighbor, of course, is that I want you to draw the energy line, a different energy, from the sixth plane to the fifth plane. It is a longer time. And then I want you to take this energy from the seventh and I want you to make little nuclei, and then around the nuclei I want you to wrap the energy of this level here [sixth plane]. Will you do that. Let's begin. Consult your neighbor. I want you to understand what happens to energy and time.[18]

FIG. 11: ENERGY OF THE SEVEN PLANES OF EXISTENCE

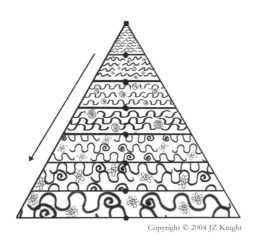

---

18 See Fig. 11: Energy of the Seven Planes of Existence.

Now when you are ready I want you to create the third level. So what happens to the energy and the time of the fourth, fifth, sixth, and seventh? What kind of body will you have out here [third plane]? How fast will it vibrate? Now what is the reason for the body? The reason is this: that if you are a spiritual being, you can only inhabit a plane if you are clothed in that which is termed the elements of the plane. So, in other words, if Spirit is born of the Void, then in order for it to exist in a level of time it has to clothe itself in a garment that is made from that time.

The Swing Movement of the Mirror Consciousness

So here we started out with that which is termed the first human beings on this planet Terra, that used to have two moons and a cloud cover. Your body was not tall, beautiful, and flawless. It was humped over, hairy, and had a small brain. But that hominid entity was the first body of a consciousness coming here [first plane] that knew only how to get here but nothing about here, because what is to know about this place other than what one creates about it? How many of you understand? So now here you are way out here. You are at the end [bottom of the triad]. So something wonderful starts to happen at the end. Take this consciousness and do this.[19] It starts to swing. This swinging is like a pendulum.

---

19 See Fig. 12: Dreaming the Dream.

Now concentrate. Remember, this is consciousness. So if the consciousness swings out here — let's say that is "yes" and let's say that is "positive" and let's say that is a dream[20] — so we are dreaming "yes."

FIG. 12: DREAMING THE DREAM

yes/positive/dream

the Now

We pause right here.[21] This is called the Now alignment. In order for this dream to become real, it has to be lined up like this, move off, experience it.

FIG. 13: THE NOW ALIGNMENT

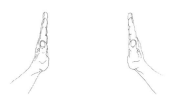

---

20 This forward motion of the hand swinging represents the positive aspect of any set of opposites. It represents good rather than bad, high rather than low, yes rather than no, the future rather than the past, etc.
21 See Fig. 13: The Now Alignment.

So now this little entity got to swinging around. And it is called the mirror consciousness that dreams, aligns, moves off, allows it to coagulate, and then moves into the coagulation as experience. Yes/Now, no/Now, positive/Now, negative/Now, future/Now, past/Now. Now this is necessary because without this entity doing this, moving off center, it can't imagine. When it moves off center, it can imagine. Once it has created the dream, it lines the dream up, closes the gap into God, pulls back, and impregnates all of time with the dream. How many of you understand?

FIG. 14: THE SWING MOVEMENT OF THE MIRROR CONSCIOUSNESS

yes/positive/future

the Now

no/negative/past

Evolution of the Human Species

Homo Erectus and Tyrannosaurus Rex

Now who were you? These wonderful, humble creatures that today you would find appalling that you once were, but that is all you needed to be. And how were you to be a part of the Earth that you helped create? How can a

172

Spirit smell a rose? How can a Spirit handle a serpent? How can a Spirit, as it were, be a tree, observe the tree? The entity who chose to come down here, which that is what you are, came into a body that was made in the same frequency of this Earth with a very small brain. You only needed a little brain, because what did you know? Not a lot. And your face was very large, animallike. Why? Because the eyes had to be large, the nostrils large, the jaw large, the limbs long, because this was the body or the vehicle for exploration. To be able to see a tree and to touch a tree, to be able to smell flora and pick flora with the body, all that was needed was a very small brain, small cranium, and large senses. Now those were your first bodies.

What is the importance of having this? Why are you stuck in it? Why can't you get out of it? And once you get out of it, how is it you avoid coming back to it? You don't ever avoid coming back to it. You will always have this body until you have developed your spiritual capacities beyond that which is termed the level of the body. In this timeline here, back here at the beginning, you started. You have all of this time in which to evolve. Now how does a person evolve? How do you change? How did your bodies change to be those beautiful entities that they are today from that which is termed its original ancestors? You know how you changed? With the Spirit of consciousness and energy flowing through an ancient brain. With that brain being able to see only what it knew existed, every time you ran into a tree, every time you fell off of a rock, and every time you experienced Tyrannosaurus Rex and his hot breath, you grew. Every time that you wanted to run for your life and couldn't run fast enough and wished that you could, you were changing that which is termed cell biology. What do you think, masters, creates the imprint on your chromosomes? What is your DNA? How does it know how to make you? Who is responsible for putting it together? Do you think your mother and father are responsible for putting you together? They were on an unconscious level because, you see, every thought you have ever thought, every fear you have ever had, every desire that you have ever had, every betrayal, every feeling, every joy, every moment you are experiencing it, it is emotion that imprints the DNA and it is emotion that changes the DNA coil. How does it change it? It imprints it.

So in your first life if you couldn't run fast enough to get rid of Tyrannosaurus Rex and you had been consumed by this entity, your last thoughts would be you wished you would have had longer legs. So you die, your body is swallowed up, becomes the dung of the earth, and you move to this level here [third plane]. And when you move to this level here, all you can remember in viewing your life was all the things that you had learned on this timeline, and then it stops. That is what you get to see up here.

So why did you get to come back and what made a difference in your life? You got to come back down here on the timeline because the woman that you impregnated the night before, this child that will be born will have longer legs in two generations. So what you want to come back with is all that you have gained up to this point. That is not a very spiritual thing, is it? Most people think in their last dying breath that they are sorry for all the things that they did and they wish they hadn't been so hard on the people that they love. Indeed they wish they could have been kinder, more giving, more understanding. They have a lot of reflection on the point of death, but that is only as a result of your evolution. The entity who was eaten by Tyrannosaurus Rex had no such reflection. The only reflection that creature had was it wished it could have outrun the monster. Now that is the last thing it desired.

Up here [third plane], that is all it will see when it gets to reflect on how far it came on the timeline. So what is it saying to its God? Not that "I am sorry that I was such an awful child" but "I wished I would have had longer legs." And what will your God do? That becomes the next generation. So you are born not into someone with short legs but into a family with long legs. Now we have a Spirit who just wants to run faster than the beasts that are chasing it, and now it is given a body that genetically has that potential. So now this being grows up, outruns, is more clever than the predators around it, and because it is, it fathers a next generation that will be exactly what he was in his life emotionally. How many of you understand? So he is going to bear children who — their life, their bodies — are going to be better equipped to live in the environment that they are in. And the souls and Spirits that inhabit those bodies will be entities that have deserved that point in evolution.

How many of you bear today both genetic and emotional traits of your parents — raise your hands — genetic and emotional traits of your parents? Both the emotional and the physical belong to genetics. How many of you have no similarities to your parents at all spiritually? Raise your hands. That means that if you are dominated by your parents in physical form, if you have inherited your mother's fear and your father's strength or your father's cowardness and your mother's guilt, if you are predisposed to be that way it is because the body genetically is creating its reality from its giver, meaning its parents. People who are weak-spirited never override this genetic destiny. In other words, like I said at the beginning this morning, their Spirit energy is being consumed by the genetics of the body. The genetics of the body is living off the spiritual energy, and the entity who is supposed to be here to learn has learned nothing.

Now imagine ten and a half million years. How long do you live, sixty years, seventy years, one hundred years? How many lifetimes, an average of eighty years, can be lived in ten and a half million years? A lot. How many of you say a lot? A lot, eh? You know, the entities say you are an old soul or you are a young soul. No, all souls were created at the same time. How many of you think you have lived two lives? There is no one in here that has lived two lives. You have lived thousands of them.

Now does it make logical sense that your forefathers and foremothers, who were apelike in appearance, evolved to Homo erectus — the hominids evolved to Homo erectus — and then from Homo erectus to Neanderthal? Is there a reason why these creatures changed? What was the reason?

Did people evolve because people had adversity? Students, did people evolve because they had problems? How many of you have evolved in this lifetime because of the difficulties you went through? So be it.

Now is it fair then to say that then your forefathers and foremothers had a lot of difficulty and they had a lot of problems? How many of you would agree? Well, you should because you are the product of their resolve, what you are today. Now these two levels of consciousness, you came from the godhood because you have a mandate and the mandate says make known the unknown. That is the only law there is, make known the unknown. That is what the Void said to its creation here, "Make of me whatever you want. Be the creator. I give you whatsoever you desire. There is no right and wrong; there is only evolution. There is only creativity."

So now we have learned that this little entity here [Point Zero], though as powerful as it was, had to move all over the Void to finally realize it had gone nowhere. And we now call that entity God. God has most certainly evolved from those days. Now it has a coherent lifeform; it has a coherent vacuum of time. Indeed this is the playground in which we are to fulfill the law of make known the unknown. When we first came into our bodies, you and I, we didn't know anything other than what we had gained in previous incarnations in this time-flow. And so if it was our first lifetime, we knew nothing and all we had to teach us was our environment and the adversity of our environment and the need, as it were, of being trapped in the physical body, to survive in that body.

But after the first lifetime we started learning. And what were we contributing to this lifeline? We were contributing thought. We were endowed with a mechanism that could take a stream of consciousness because, remember, consciousness, the brain, and the mind are all different. Consciousness is the stream from God. The brain is the receiver, for it takes that consciousness and creates it into memorable, neurological thought and it can freeze that thought in the form of memory. Memory in creation is like gathering blocks of stone in which to build a hovel from. Thought in the brain, collected in the form of knowledge, allows you to re-create thought-forms, that if they are held in the forefront of the brain's neocortex will be the lawgivers that collapse energy into form. So the brain had to evolve to fit our level of need.

So what are we gaining out of this? If we realize that we need longer legs to outrun Tyrannosaurus Rex, that is a learning; that is creation. Just the need through adversity to be better, that then lays the groundwork in the body for a more evolved body. And what does it do for your spiritual self? It has made you realize that in order to live here, you must re-create yourself. Here we are, going ten and a half million years. You have all lived as men, women. You have all been children, fathers, mothers, sistren, brethren. You have all been slain, eaten, burned, died peacefully, drowned. You have all met your death in a myriad of uncreative ways. You have done it all.

Intervention of the Gods

Four hundred and fifty-five thousand years ago, approximately here on this timeline, something wonderful happened right here [first plane]. The beings, that while you were still up here on the seventh level, were already descending. You see, no one descended at the same time; everyone went differently. And yet it was up to each one of you to create this. You still have beings today that are alive and well on the fifth plane and they have never gone any lower. Perhaps in the next two hundred years they will make their way down here; perhaps they will never come. But that is all they have known. Some of you have called them angels. You call them that because they have an utter innocence about this place. They have no judgment, no good and bad. They understand it not. They only understand love. But they have never lived here. They have never been a Christ because they have never embodied God in flesh and blood.

While you were about here [fourth plane], we already had entities that had already come down here billions and billions of years ago who were on this timeline in this three-dimensional matter vibrating at 8.2 hertz that had already moved down this timeline. Now when they moved down here [first plane] and they got past this point here [third plane], they were building a spiritual reality that was moving way up here [fourth plane]. In other words, their reality was happening this fast [fourth-plane time] in a body this slow [first-plane body]. How many of you understand? So they went on down this way and started gradually getting brighter and brighter, and they exist about right here [fourth plane]. They are your brothers and sisters. They live on various different planets and most of them live on the interior of those planets, since all orbiting orbs are hollow. They surpassed you now. Four hundred and fifty-five thousand years ago every one of you in this room came up against this timeline [first plane]. You finally got this far. So how far were you? Well, you knew you were male and female. You would cohabitate for the sake of bearing young. The females were dominant in the tribes, since they were that which is termed the culture's leaders. The males provided the food for the family. We had sort of a moral household.

At this particular point this group of entities called the Gods came back. And they came down here and they realized you need a little help, and that with as far as you had advanced, you hadn't advanced very far. So what did they do? They mercifully interacted in your timeline of evolution. Now about here [first plane] you possessed a small brain, large facial features. This small brain ended up being the reptilian brain, the midbrain, up to the corpus callosum. So, in other words, the brain that was contained right here did not contain the yellow brain of the neocortex. At this point in your evolution you were very psychic. You could send messages far and wide because your brain operated in infrared, which is called the psychic realm. But you had a primitive brain.

These entities came along, took you and commingled their seed with yours, so they bred into your body their experiences.

Remember I asked you how many of you wore your parents' identity as well as their emotional identity, and many of you raised your hands? When these elected beings finished commingling with all of you, you drastically changed as a culture. Not only did you start to lose body hair but you gained in proportional height. Your skeleton changed. You lost two ribs and gained an enormous brain. Your facial features became less defined than the overexaggerated hominid's facial features.

Now why did they do this? Because they are your brothers and sisters. They are Gods from the same Source, who are ahead of you in evolution. They also used you as servants, which would make a great amount of logic. Since your capacity for evolutionary knowledge had not been gained, since you were only at this timeline here, you didn't know all that they knew. So what were your tasks? Your tasks were to commingle, cohabitate, and to live with them. They in turn taught you psychology. They taught you art. They taught you mathematics, astronomy. It was they who imbued within you a sense of culture and, moreover, a sense of that which is termed dynamic self. But how great were you? You had a large neocortex, large but barely used, because the experience that it took to give you that genetic body, as a Spirit you had not lived. So it would be as if your children were walking around in their parents' clothing. The clothing fits but it is still a child who is exhibiting itself in the body. How many of you understand? Now when that happened, it happened 455,000 years ago. Would you write that down.

The genetic manipulation of humanity by the Gods happened 455,000 years ago.

Now those Gods, who became the legends of biblical texts, created your bodies, created my body, interacted, and went on about their life. What did it do for all of us? What it did is that it brought us to 455,000 years ago in a holding pattern on the timeline. In other words, what do you call today in your Julian calendar? It is nearing 2000. According to that calendar, it is past the year 2000. So where are you two thousand years from this point? You haven't changed because you are in a holding pattern, so you have been reincarnating over and over and over again, coming back with the same amount of spiritual growth as you left behind the last lifetime. And what is that to say? That humanity leveled off forty thousand years ago and the cranium of the human being from forty thousand years ago to today hasn't changed. So it means that as spiritual people you keep reincarnating into a genetic line that you have yet to use all of its machinery.

Forty Thousand Years of Evolutionary Stillness

Now this seems that this introduction, to be very tedious, but it can be somewhat interesting when you begin to understand where your roots go back to, and it is important for you to understand this. Before you can go on and start creating reality, you need some answers to your questions. You don't use all of your brain. You use less than a tenth of it. Less than a tenth of the massive neocortex means that there is a great deal of potential that you have never actualized. Even Einstein when he perished had not used all of his brain, had not mapped that which is termed new ideas and new theories, and fell short of that which is termed developing the discovery of new mathematics to describe what he was seeing in a unified vision.

So if then you are a spiritual being who is actually behind your nature, it would then begin to make a great deal of logic to you that the laziness inside of you and the impatience inside of you is a primitive Spirit in a very advanced body. Does that make logic to you? Because the geniuses amongst you — And all that a genius is is one who expands the borders of its mind, and that mind is everything. If we understand, then the reason you haven't evolved a great deal in ten and a half million years is because you are still back 455,000 years ago and the body leveled off 40,000 years ago. And you have yet to use the capacity of your body. You have yet to develop your spiritual self that it can operate this body as a fine-tuned instrument of God. Now what did you do last lifetime? Were you in the technical revolution? Did you die in World War II? Was your home bombed? Did you die of famine in Ireland? Did you die of the plague? How many children do you have and where are they today? What did you contribute last lifetime? Can't remember.

In this life and why you came here to learn was "How do I live to the greatest of my spiritual potential, thereby using my body to its greatest potential?" And do you have Gods in your genes? Indeed you do. Do you have an advanced intelligence that you are carrying around in you? Indeed you do. Are you the children of a superior race? Many of them. But the race itself is only as great as the intelligence that created it and that, of course, comes back to God, the dreamer of all origins.

At this time the reason that you are unhappy with your life is because you are at the end of your ability to dream reality. You let everything do it for you. You go to the motion pictures and you let someone else act out an adventure while you stand by and watch. You listen to someone else sing you a melody while your mouth stays quiet. You swoon at someone else's poetry. You marvel at someone else's artwork. You let someone else's genius plug you in, for convenience. And is it any wonder that you are bored and that you need entertainment, because it is not coming out of you. If you are Gods — and you most certainly are — and if consciousness and energy creates the nature of reality, perhaps the problem that we have here is the inability to believe in oneself, of its capability. And perhaps you have inherited that gene through your parents. Most parents never believed they were greater than the stock in which they came from.

So here is what you have been doing for forty thousand years. You have had this consciousness out here swinging violently back and forth. How fickle are you? Do one moment you approve and the next moment you disapprove? Is one moment you like and the next moment you don't like? And what about your future? What future? Oh, that future. Isn't your future just more of thinking about your past? Well, if that is so then, your future is stuck back here, and so this, that someone told you that this no longer existed, that this was out here. When the Gods left, they went to heaven and they left you here, and you believed that. And so belief, being the creator of reality, put to bed this God [God within] and put the God of your choice out there.

What about Jehovah? Jehovah is nothing more than an advanced entity who was highly insecure and warlike, who hated his sister. How about the Lord God Id? What is the Lord God Id? They were Gods, beings, people that had problems just like you are having problems. But somewhere they told you that they were lord and someone got it mixed up that lord meant boss.

And so the God that you are supposed to line up with, create a dream and give it to and then move off of that dream so it can manifest in energy — that imagination coagulates energy, that is what brings on experience — you are stuck because you think it is out there instead of in here. So for forty thousand years you have been doing this every lifetime. And what does that mean? That means that you have gone to school, you have learned everything that the culture has to give you, and you are bored, and you have nothing else to contribute because you don't know how to dream the dream, line it up, collapse time, bring it back, have energy collapsed into visual form, and then experience it. So now we have this going on, which needs to stop. We have everyone moving a little bit off of this timeline and then they die, go up here [third plane], take a look at what they have, and they are coming back to this timeline. You are stuck. No one can get past their image.

Only a few are breaking away and going out here [fourth plane]. And as they move past this God problem, they get out here and they start becoming spiritual, and they are reaching deep within the Source and manifesting it down here [first plane]. Who is a Christ? One who finishes the timeline and goes home. Turn to your neighbor and explain.

CHAPTER FOUR
Energy,
the Handmaiden
of Consciousness

Runners

So the advanced students are mumbling amongst themselves that you are getting a lot of information. You are. And I have bypassed many details that are a nice setup for your future learning. But I like to do this: In the deliverance of that which is termed this philosophy, I am sending you runners to help manifest it for you so that you see it as a truth. So be it. Now what is a runner? An entity who brings your post is a runner. An entity who rings your "tele" is a runner, someone who is interacting with you or creating a situation in which the result of that interaction brings forth a specific philosophy that can be experienced in truth. So I am going to send you a lot of runners. And the only reason that I am giving you what I am giving you today is that this year in your time is leading up to some quite marvelous discoveries and that when they happen, you are going to remember sitting in this audience and hearing all of this. And I daresay you will be looking for your papers and pencils and you will be grabbing someone to draw these little pictures, timelines and such.

Energy, a Wave and a Particle

Now we are going to leave this for a moment and we are going to talk about energy. How many of you have heard that energy is related to the aspect of the serpent? Raise your hands. How many of you have learned that energy is related to knowledge that is represented in the serpent? Would you raise your hands. So be it. Well, it is called that because this is what a wave of energy looks like. The energy just doesn't start and just end. It begins with a thought and ends in a thought. Two levels of consciousness contain energy. Now energy moves like this; it undulates. According to whatever level consciousness is being extracted into the experience tells us what kind of energy to expect. If we have a very advanced intelligence, indeed if we have that which is termed an advanced level of consciousness, then what you start to feel from them are bursts of this energy. Moreover, entities who have the ability to manifest their thoughts have this sort of energy radiating from them. If we have entities who are slow and slothlike, who are definitely on this timeline, who don't care very much about life, their energy is going to be like this: long, undulated energy, preceded and ending with thoughts and conclusions.

But what does this mean, these wave lines? When you say that an entity has wonderful energy, what do you mean when you say that? Or what is it that you mean when you say, "I felt a very harmful energy coming off of that person"? How many of you have made such statements in your life? Raise your hands. Now that means that energy is a virgin, but it is a carrier wave of a thought. It is thought in motion. So if a person has a very harmful energy, you will feel it because it is their consciousness flowing through their brain emanating in the form of a mind, that that mind rides this field. And when you pick it up in your brain back here [lower cerebellum], your brain deciphers this energy into fields of collective thought. In other words, it weighs it: Is this good or is this bad, good or bad? Energy is neither good nor bad.

188

Energy is neither positive nor negative. It is both. And nothing is good and bad as seen in the light of all eternity. But in order for you to be creators and Gods like I said that you are, then there must be something in you that would ring forth a divineness. In other words, there has got to be something more than digestion that seems to equate to your divine nature. So what is it?

Well, there is a word that is vastly underused and misused, and it is called that which is hidden, that which is hidden. That which is hidden is sacred knowledge. But what is that sacred knowledge? The sacred knowledge is that until you can uncover that which is hidden, you will never gain the sacred knowledge. But in a philosophical commentary on that we would say then that that which is hidden simply means that inside every wave of energy is a carrier field of mind and that energy is both a particle and a wave and that when it starts here, it starts with an idea or a thought.[1] When it is released, it is moved into a field and concludes as reality.

So look at the space between you and your partner. Just turn around and gauge the space between the two of you. What is existing in that space? Can you feel your partner's energy? How many of you can feel your partner's energy? Are they dead or alive? What is it that you are not seeing? What about between you and I, what about this space? This space is called that which is hidden. It is the invisible. And the invisible simply says that the atmosphere around you, this atmosphere around you, is a field of energy that looks just like this and that in this field of energy we have energy and potentials.[2]

Touch your neighbor on the shoulder. Now as far as it takes to touch your neighbor on the shoulder is the only distance required to go back to the seventh level. Everything

1 See Fig. 15: Collapse of the Energy Wave into a Particle.
2 Ibid.

189

that you want in your life — fabulous wealth, radiant youth, health, longevity — the energy that it takes to bring that about in your life takes less of a field than it takes to touch your neighbor's shoulder. So do it again and contemplate that. That is that which is hidden. Now this atmosphere down here in linear time, the atmosphere in the room, those fields that make up the elements of the Earth, the solar system, and the galaxy, they are all made up of the same energy field in different stages of evolution. But it is the same field in different stages. Down here [first plane], right where you are, contains all of this [seven levels of reality].

The Observer Collapses the Fields of Energy

Now what is divine in you? What is divine in you is consciousness and energy being frozen through the mechanics of a human brain. Why is that important? Because if you are surrounded with this — and you must be surrounded with these unraveling or raveling or tightening down; this is all around you — then what is it that affects this field? Thought. It is called the Observer. And where is the Observer? The Observer is inside of your head.

Now if you have the power to create reality, it means that you have the power to affect this field, this field right here [the bands around the body]. And what is this field? All of this [seven levels] in different stages all the way back up to here [Point Zero]. And what is it about you that can affect the field? If you are this entity here [Observer] and you are having a thought right here [frontal lobe], then you are affecting this field around you. How do you do that? All matter, all mass — what you are sitting on, what you are wearing, what your body is made up of — is made up of

190

subatomic particles. How many of you have heard of atoms? Do you not find it interesting that atoms and Adam sound the same, the first man, the first particle? Those particles — What do you think an atom looks like? It has a nuclei; correct? Don't go to sleep. What is composed in the nuclei? Protons. What else? What else? What is inside a proton? Quark. So where did they come from? Right here [sixth plane] is the quark field. Down here is the proton field [fifth plane]. Down here [fourth plane] is the closure of the nuclei. And all down here [first, second, and third planes] is the racing of matter and antimatter, what is called electrons and positrons. So all an atom is is the availability of potential.

If you unfurl an atom at its nucleus level, you have an atomic bomb. How many of you know the power of an atomic bomb? Isn't it interesting that the energy comes from that which is hidden? The smaller the particle, the more powerful the energy. Did it ever occur to you, beginners, where that energy came from? Perhaps the energy that is unfurled in the splitting of the nucleus is really splitting apart this coiled energy that has been tightened down through the slowing of time.[3] Does that make logic to you? Is that a nice philosophy? Because if you rupture it, the kind of energy that you get is the sort of energy that is common on these levels. And that is what an atom is. All it is is that which is hidden, seven levels of reality in a particle.

FIG. 15: COLLAPSE OF THE ENERGY WAVE INTO A PARTICLE

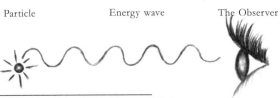

Particle   Energy wave   The Observer

3 See Fig. 11: Energy of the Seven Planes of Existence.

Now what affects the atom? Why? If all matter is made up of atoms, how did it get there? All an atom is is atmospheres of other planes coagulated and closed. Are they sensitive? Well, if we have a nuclei here and then we have the outer shell here and we have orbiting electrons, positrons, that then means that every electron that moves around this atom moves around this atom because we allow it to move around the atom. And how is it that we allow? We take it for granted. In other words, you are the Observer. If you focused on this particular particle, this atom, if you focused on its electrons, you could reverse the spin of the electrons around this atom. Why could you do that? Because that is your divine nature. If you are supposed to evolve and to make known the unknown, what is the faculty in you that is responsible for doing it? It is focused consciousness. When you have a thought and if you were to focus on this atom by adding electrons or taking them away, you would change the nature of its energy.

Why? The field that exists between you and I you don't see, and because you don't see it it is doing this.[4] It is in motion, momentum. The moment you stop to look at the atmosphere between you and I, you start to see little lights. How many of you have seen those? You have? Well, so someone told you that was just something happening with your eyeball? That is not anything happening with your eyeball. Those little lights are, in effect, this energy wave collapsing into a particle with an orbital light, which is called the electron. The moment you stop focusing on the invisible field, the lights disappear and then all you see is what you are looking at in the near distance, you to I, I to you. As long as you ignore this field, it stays inert, meaning you don't

---

4 Moving as a wave of energy. See Fig. 15: Collapse of the Energy Wave into a Particle.

activate it, so it stays status quo. The moment that you focus on what is hidden, you unveil what is hidden.

Now consciousness and energy creates the nature of reality. Any solid object is made solid by the creator of that object, and the creator of that object agrees that it is solid, so it stays solid. But the truth is when you go to sleep tonight, your bedroom will disappear or it will fuzz out and the light in your refrigerator will fade, because the moment that you go to sleep you are no longer observing your room, and the moment you no longer observe your room, it fuzzes out. How many of you agree? That is the way it is.

Now then how is it that you can open one little eyelid and gaze around the room and see everything the way it is supposed to see? Who determines that it is going to be that way? How many of you say you do? You are correct. But what if you woke up one morning and saw that you were in the twenty-third universe? What would happen to your room? Well, it depends. You see, this is a trap, because if you woke up thinking you were in the twenty-third universe and knew absolutely that you were there, you would be there. It would be very clear. The moment you asked yourself what happened to my room, you would wake up. Have you got it? Now you are so powerful that whatever you put here [frontal lobe], no matter if it is trash or divinity, it affects energy.

Whatsoever you think is either freeing energy up from its past or collapsing it into its future. So now I want you to take your arms and do this.[5] This is energy. Come on. When we allow it to be, it is moving like this.[6] What happens

---

5 Energy undulates like the movement of a serpent. Ramtha demonstrates this movement with his arm and the palm of his hand open. When the energy wave is collapsed into a particle, the undulating movement stops and the hand closes tight into a fist, which represents the particle.

6 See Fig. 15: Collapse of the Energy Wave into a Particle.

when we focus on it? That is it. It becomes mass. What happens when we forget about it? Party time. This is the way it works. Now down here you have a fabulous atmosphere of all these potentials, but what happens and the reason people stay on the same timeline incarnation after incarnation after incarnation is because what they have done is they have given their conscious power over to the needs of their body. And so what they do, they are born into a body who is genetically predisposed to be a certain way. And so they allow the body to grow up and have its way. The body is on genetic automatic pilot. Are you with me? How many of you are still with me?

Now as long as the body is on automatic pilot, it means that everything is set for your life. Nothing is moving in and out of it; it is all set. So you go day in and day out allowing your body to create reality. Now what does your body know about creating reality? It knows only to survive and that it needs food to survive and that it needs sleep and that it needs to be urinated, it needs to have its waste removed from it, and after rest it is rejuvenated. That is what it knows. That is called survival. Most people, although highly educated, never get beyond the level of survival in their life. They never move into free space of creativity so magic, as it is termed, never happens to them. If the body and the brain are operating on a day-to-day life, then what is tomorrow going to bring? You know what tomorrow is going to bring because you have lived millions of tomorrows, so your tomorrow is just your past. And if you go to school and you learn all of this knowledge, all it is is memorized theory. And the only reason you learn that is so that you can make a living to feed your body. How many of you understand?

So now if you are magnetically attracted to another person, you may never have been ever attracted to this Spirit before but you are attracted to this body type. And why? Because the body type is equal to the body type and complements the one that you have. There is a magnetic resonance involved. So you have relationships and you have copulation; then you bear children. What kind of children are you going to have? You are going to have children that are slightly improved from you, but are they born with an ability to intuitively create or are they needing to be educated in order to create? So now how many lives do you think you have lived like this to where you have just allowed your body to dictate your life? Infinite.

So why is magic so important? Because magic never happens openly to those who are living a life dictated by their genetics. Why? Because it is the Observer in us, it is the Spirit in us, that has the power to reveal what is hidden, not the body. But if we are weak and live only for our material self, we never develop the focus necessary to unveil the distance between you and I into a reality. So you want to get away from this life? You think it is so terrible? It is a blessing because no matter if you die tonight, you are going to be born back into this existence. And what kind of parents are you going to come back to? Those that are equal to your level of acceptance now. And so then you are going to be born again. This body and this brain are going to die, and all of its cognitive memory will perish with it. And so now you are in a brand-new body that you have to go about learning again and are a little uncertain about its genetic programming.

So you won't remember this life. And you think this is bad and you want to get out of this life, but you are just jumping into another fire. And do you know how many times you have been doing it? For eons. Let us say safely that you have been on a static progress since forty thousand years ago. And so who is responsible for all of this technology? A few people. And why did they bring about such technology? Because those beings had an ability that you are going to learn, you are going to be inspired, and you are going to develop. It is the ability of imagination to take knowledge and put it together in building blocks of thoughtful creativity and then to be possessed of that thought. If you are possessed of such an imagination for a period of time and your level of acceptance is that you accept it, that thought is going to affect this field and what used to be will dissolve and move into a liquid state. Imagination will re-effect this state and it will coagulate, not as it used to be but as it will be.

Spiritual people are the people who have led discovery. Spiritual people have been the philosophers of old that have given to you and your generations the groundwork of a philosophy that always talks about what is hidden within the individual. And it has only been a few sparkled through every civilization that have made an indent on the culture as a whole. But you were not responsible for the microchip. You were not responsible for the physics of the microchips. You were not the creator of rupturing the nuclei of an atom, nor were you the entity who created telepathic uses in the form of a telephone. You did not create the microwave. You did not create the television. You did not create the automachine. You did not weave the carpet that you are sitting upon. So what did you do? You worked for them.

Now when we wake up consciously, there comes a moment that we know. I had my moment and you will have yours. And in that moment we are suddenly separated from our ignorance and uplifted into a mist of freedom. It is called knowingness. The moment that you know that your focused thought affects life, when you really know that is the moment that you will start to take care to discipline your thinking, because if this runs away with you it will destroy you. If the Spirit is awakened in it, it will liberate you. Joy is not being physical. Joy is being the lord of the physical, not its slave.

So if you have created everything in your life, people, you are responsible for everything you have done for yourself. You are responsible for your successes and your failures, and it was you who determined they were successes or failures. If you were the person responsible for your happiness or your depression, it was you who chose to feel those ways, and it was as simple as that and always has been.

The moment that you know that your mind can shift this and accelerate it, the moment you know that, your life changes in that moment. And how does it change? It says, "Now I know the power was within me, that whatsoever I think, I create. My reality is only equal to my runaway thinking. But what if I were to sit down, still, in one moment, and ask myself what want I from this life? What is it that I have never known? What is it I have never experienced? What about myself? If I use less than a tenth of my brain, what must I do to activate the rest of it? And what far potential would I possess if indeed I could do that?"

Now you make a list. What would you want to do? If your life could be longer and you could change anything according to what you are thinking and according to your acceptance, how different would you be today? Vastly different, vastly different, because at that moment then, you would understand that the brain operates on flashes of pictures, holograms, and that every time they flash we call this thinking, and that every time it flashes it occupies this space right here [frontal lobe], and every time it flashes from this point here it is affecting this field.

What if then I could draw a thought, and what if I could hold that thought right here for a deliberate period of time, would the same law apply to a deliberate use of the Observer's principle in creating reality? Indeed it will, because the moment you hold it here with utter acceptance is the moment you change your timeline. Everything starts to change into a flux. What you dream here, what you hold here [frontal lobe], when you get up your life will start to fall apart and you will say, "This is not what I saw." Yes, it is what you saw because as everything falls apart, what we are saying is if we could dismantle the particles in a table, the table would disappear and what we would have would be a radiant light-field where the table once was. That is change, is it not? So how constricted is your life? The life that you have had on this timeline has been stuck and keeps reincarnating itself. What is beyond this place? Is there more to live, more to be, more to know? There is indeed. But what must you do to get in the timeline? You have to dissolve the past, because everyone in this room thinks in terms of their future based on their past. And what holds you there? Guilt, negativity, fear, and afraid to change. So what happens when you focus on something wonderful in your life? A lot of things in your life are going to fall apart. Why? Because the energy that holds them together must be liberated so that what you are wanting can be re-formed.

Being God Is about Giving Life

It is enough for this day. I want to end this day in saying to you what you have long heard but never understood: God is love. What does that mean? Say it to yourself. What does that mean? Love is the act of always giving. It is not about taking. So God, this entity here — this entity here [Point Zero] — gives and holds steadfast the principle of life that can be explored. When you love yourself, it will not be in a passionate embrace. It will not be about consoling yourself with poetic words. What is love is the act of giving, to give. God never takes, only gives. Life has been expanded from this moment. It has never been contracted. God is incapable of judgment. God is incapable of judging you, hating you, condemning you. There is no such thing. There is only allowing.

To know what love is is to open up and to give. It is like breaking down the dam of water that is held back by the dam. It is a giving of consciousness. When you learn to love yourself, you will learn to love yourself as such. You will give to yourself not things but freedom. You will cease judging yourself as being a failure or a success. You will cease feeling guilty about your past, because you never have a future as long as you are anchored in guilt. You will give up your enemies because when you give them up, they give you up. That is loving yourself. It takes an enormous amount of energy to have an enemy and to keep them always in your mind.

Loving yourself is forgiving you. And say to yourself, "In the light of all eternity what was this action worth, to hold me back forever or to expand me so I can see over the hill?" God is love because God gives you every day of your life and supports you with the energy necessary to create life. And you have your time and you have your season. When you can do the same with yourself, then love is born in you. Don't expect people to love you. They are incapable of it. Expect yourself to love you. And the way you love you is to give to you freedom, peace, and when you take that and give it to yourself, you then usher it to other people. Give to them. Give to them.

Give people room to make mistakes. So what? They are on the verge of wisdom. Virtue is not the abstinence of life; it is doing it in life. Give people a wide berth. Don't look for them to make a mistake. Love them, allow them. Don't hold someone in your power and play games with them. Give them freedom and be honest and truthful with them. And the honesty is that "I am giving to you what I most crave in myself." Forgive your parents if they didn't raise you properly. No one knows how to raise anyone properly. But celebrate that you have life and that they gave you life. Give. Give. Don't take. Don't take. Give, and in the act of giving you will become God. When you are merciful, your God is merciful. When you are forgiving, your God is forgiving. How can you expect to forgive yourself and not forgive your enemies? Only when you have forgiven yourself do you have the wisdom to enact that power towards others.

People who are takers are victims, and you all have been takers. You think life owes you something. You think your parents owe you something. You think your friends owe you something. You think your lover owes you something. No one owes you anything. You are a taker, not a giver. If you are a taker, then you do not embody God. If you are a giver, you embody the divine power within you because there is no end to the resource.

Tonight I want you, after you have left here and eaten and had much frivolity, I want you to have a peaceful time tonight before you go into your slumber and I want you to be disciplined about it. I want you to sit down and think of three things that you would like to have happen in your life, just three things, a dream — it can be anything — it can be a more glorious Spirit, it can be having lucid life as lucid dreaming, it can be fabulous wealth. It can be anything as long as you accept it. Now if you don't accept what you are putting down, you shall not have.

So go back into your room of dreams and go looking for something you lost along the way. And most of you lost it when you were children. Go back and find something that you would like to have happen to you, but make certain it is within the realm of your acceptance. And then you write it out, draw a picture of it. When you are finished, I want you to contemplate yourself, and the point I want you to focus on is what you want you to change about yourself. And everything is possible. There is no such thing as permanent addiction to the past. It is only temporary. You focus on your lack, your doubt — anything — your sickness, and then write it out. What are three things you want to change about your life? Write it out and then draw a picture of it. That is all I want you to do.

And then before you go to your slumber — don't watch television — read, so that you go to sleep with lofty thoughts in your mind. And what is it that you need to read? Read about quantum mechanics. Read about creating reality. Read about the concept of another life and who will you be in that other life. Give yourself food for your Spirit — not your body but your Spirit — and go to sleep with that in your brain.

Then you be back here tomorrow morning, same time, in your seats, with a smile on your face because tomorrow is a brand-new day. And you are going to change by tomorrow so that when you leave my audience, you will walk away from here and you will miss this place, and especially me, and you will feel lifted. That is part of the journey. That is how it starts.

Now I love you. How is it I can do that? Because I give to you and because you are why I am manifested the way that I am. And what is there about you to love? That which I was. You are forgotten Gods, utterly. You are in a state of amnesia about your own divinity. You are, for the most part, superstitious and dogmatic. What I have taught you today is very simple. Most certainly it is complex when we understand it in biological terms. And it may be disturbing and complex when we talk about the hidden being made manifest as energy, but it will become clear.

There is a lot you don't know. I would never guard my ignorance so jealously, and I certainly would not put up barriers of doubt to keep my ignorance intact. So be here tomorrow open-minded. I love you. You have already done the worst you could ever do to yourself. There is nothing worse than what you have already done. And you will never be possessed or cultlike, nor will you be a follower, nor will you be brainwashed. You have already been that. You are that. You will never go backwards; you will only go forwards. So tomorrow we manifest reality, joy, and a new discipline. So be it.

I salute the God within you. That is the meaning of this gesture.[7] You are excused. So be it. That is all.

---

[7] Ramtha salutes the God within every person by joining his hands as if in prayer, pointing to his seventh seal, and bowing to them.

CHAPTER FIVE
Effects of the Teachings
on the Students of the Great Work

Your God Has Never Judged You

I salute you from the Lord God of my being to the Lord God of your being. Let's have a drink, eh?

O my beloved God,
that which has created me
and given unto me life,
awaken in me
my passion to know.
Give back my power,
that I may manifest
a journey,
a path,
to enlightenment.
So be it.
To life.

Be seated. Oh, beginners, how be you this day? How many of you realize you learned something yesterday? You did? Why did you come back? Turn to your neighbor and tell them why you came back today. Confession is excellent for the soul.

Now I listened to some of your conversations last night. I like to eavesdrop on my beginners because their opinion, I can read what their words are saying and I know what their thoughts are saying. So I want to answer a few of your questions out loud today. Now I am not mad. Two different groups discussed my demeanor. My demeanor looks like that I am angry and mad. I am not angry and mad. I just speak with inflection of my voice. I want you to know that if where I am would be that which is termed dreary and remorseful and angry, I should say to you straightaway don't go there; stay here. It is not that way. To be that which is termed God within is to be light of heart — light, joyful — joyful, not artificially joyful but there is an ease about life instead of a burden about it.

Now listen. One fine morning you are going to wake up and realize, as it were, what I have taught you. And you won't sit there struck dumb. You will start laughing and it will come from some wonderful place that you can't stop. And you are going to laugh and laugh and laugh because you will see the mirth that lies on the other side of this serious human attitude that everything is oppressive and everything is dreadful. I tell you, the God that I love never judged anyone. It is a giving entity. It is a source. It never says to you, "Well, you want it but you can't have it." It never says to you, "You should do penance before you get it." It never says to you, "Say you are sorry; then I will give it to you." They should take Yeshua ben Joseph off of that cross. What a sad sight. It is to make you feel guilty.

I tell you, the God that you are learning about is everlasting life and a life that is so full that you don't even have the mind yet to begin to recognize how much there is yet to experience. Don't you know that you have experienced the most rotten part of life? If you are stuck in a reincarnation loop and you have been living the same attitude, just imagine — imagine, you sitting here — imagine a thousand lifetimes being the same you in different bodies.

How boring. No wonder you are not invited back home.

Your ability to change is in a moment. Imagine what you have not learned. Imagine what you don't know. You have been stuck, reincarnated, on the same behavioral pattern, different bodies, the same old attitude. You can't do any worse than you have already done. You know, there are some entities who say that all you will learn that life is not worth anything and it is all right to kill and all of that stuff. Let me tell you something. If you have been alive or been coming back here for at least ten and a half million years, don't you think that the probability that you have already done that is fairly great? I would suggest that it is probably the odds of ten and a half million to one that you have already murdered someone else and then of course been murdered, and that you have been scoundrels, derelicts, you have been rapers, you have been kings and queens, paupers, slaves, servants, holy men, sinful men, virtuous women, whoring women. You have been everything. So what makes you think that what is yet to know is more of the same stuff? It doesn't get worse after this; it gets greater.

So, you know, let's not ponder, as someone else suggested, that everything is all right. Let's not say that this teaching gives you permission to be bad. You have already been bad. What the teaching does is to tell you to realize that and to say what are you going to do with the rest of your life? Are you going to be the same old predictable person every single day, so much so that you don't even love yourself, and if you met yourself and yourself asked you to have a relationship, you would run away from yourself?

Knowledge Gives Us Hope

What are you going to do the rest of your life? What are you going to do? Are you going to continue to work the rest of your life? Are you going to continue to get stoned the rest of your life? Are you going to continue to live off of other people the rest of your life? Are you going to continue to feel sorry for yourself for the rest of your life? Are you going to make people feel bad about your existence, your mother, your father? What are you going to do? Are you going to have children, make them feel bad about being born? What are you going to do till, oh, say, the day you die? What is on your agenda?

The teachings, as a master appropriately replied, give us hope, give us hope because first it gives us knowledge to put down our ignorance. And don't you know that superstition comes out of ignorance? Think of all the cultures who are superstitious of walking under a ladder. Think of all the cultures that are superstitious about blaspheming God. Think of all the cultures that are superstitious about virginity. Think about all of the cultures that absolutely believe in blood sacrifice. Think about them. The teachings put to rest superstition and ignorance.

What you are going to learn today is that which is termed a marriage of science, theology, and me. You are going to learn practical aspects about your brain, what part responds to what. You are going to get to answer a question of where do I get the body that I move into after the death of this body. Where does it come from? How do I manifest it? You are going to be answering questions to yourself of why are some people psychic and other people are not. This isn't new knowledge. In fact the new knowledge of today is pitifully impoverished and for the most part is intended to be, because governments do not survive when people are all-knowing and aware. Commercialism doesn't survive when people have the power to create reality. So in this culture there is a downplay of the divinity in man and an intent conspiracy on robbing everyone of individual thought. That is why everyone is intent on making everyone the same, believe the same, act the same, buy the same products, look the same, because in sameness there is control. In individuality there is unpredictability. Governments must hold themselves together with a populace that they can corner and catalog. And governments only survive as power when everyone agrees. But what about when you had — What if America, this place, were all enlightened to the level of Christ? Would we still have Republicans and Democrats? Would you have a national debt? Would you? Would you have — what is it called? — Medicare?

So how about the people who have an agenda about keeping a government together, is it to their advantage to do away with superstition and dogma? It is not to their advantage. It divides and conquers the people, and they are the people who keep them in control. Now this teaching is not secular. This teaching is about a brain, a spiritual body, and levels of development. The teaching says to you, very blatantly today, you have in you everything you need to change your life. Now is there someone here, including me, going to make you change? No. You are forgotten Gods. You may be forgotten but you are still Gods. And the only entities that have forgotten that that is a truth is you. So being a God then and being that you have a responsibility to make known the unknown, you have your own will. After you learn every knowledge that you are going to learn today, if you do not use it, that is your will. That doesn't mean you are right or you are wrong. It simply is a choice. But knowledge frees us from fear, the fear that we can't do the work, and it fears — The future suddenly becomes predictable instead of unpredictable.

Another question, now we know I am not mad and God is not mad. Why do I talk this way? Why not? Why not? This is a vocal cord and a brain. And the way that the brain responds to the vocal cords, why not, why not talk this way? Another question is that I seem to be loud. I am. I am. I am not Jesus Christ. And who is to say that he wasn't loud? He was very loud.

Truth Is Philosophy in Action

Another question. You are not certain you are coming back today because you don't know if it is the truth. What did I tell you about the truth? Nothing I tell you is the truth. God only knows what you know. And it is only truth when it gets to be in your way and you have to work your way through it. Then it is truth. If it never gets in your way and you never put it there, it will never be truth. It will just be another New Age teaching, and it won't be truth until you experience it. And you need a lot of truth in order to stand up to your cynical mind. You do. It doesn't do anyone any good to say you have the power to heal yourself if they don't believe it. Moreover, it doesn't do any of you any good to say you want to be wealthy. If you want to be wealthy, sit down and create a card and a picture of fabulous wealth and focus on it for an hour each day until your focus turns to being it. That is all you have to do. Then you get it. Now what you do with it, that is another focus. But unless you use it, it doesn't work and it is not going to be the truth.

So, no, I don't talk about truth. I talk about that which is termed a philosophy. It was truth for me and allowed me to emerge in this time frame to give you what I knew. Is it important that you believe in me? You don't have to believe in me; that is not a requirement. What you do need to require is to believe in yourself. And use me, you know, use me like a burning bush. Listen to what I have to say. Pick and choose out of it what is right for you. And you don't have to use it all. And if it doesn't work, then you can still use me to blame for it not working. I come in very handy in that category.

Do that until you are tired of doing it and then take your responsibility and say, "Look, if I really wanted this, I would have gotten it." That is how it is. Immaculate faith happens in a moment. Immaculate curing, healing, restoration happens in a moment. And the reason it takes so long for most of you? Because the road is paved with doubt and disbelief. Now if you can get rid of that, in a moment everything you want will fall right into place. It takes you that long to make it manifest.

You see, you are out here [first plane]. It takes a long time for something to manifest in the timeline out here. But what if your body was here [first plane] and your consciousness was here [seventh plane]? What if you had the faith of a seventh-level being? We call those beings masters. They live in a body but their mind is on the seventh level and their energy is on the seventh level, and they use that in a physical body way back here. So their body is here but their consciousness is here [seventh plane] so when they say something, that is how long it takes for it to happen [immediately]. If you are way out here [first plane] and you believe only in your stomach and you believe only in your body, your addictions, you know how long it takes for something to happen? Most of you take it out here [dream the dream] and don't even take the time to do this [align with Point Zero], too impatient, so you hang out here and your timeline is going that way.[1] Well, what about that way? That way is only the opposite of this way, which is the past. So it takes a long time.

We have people in this school who still haven't manifested what they say they really want. Why? Because that manifestation stays out here [upper four planes] instead of here [first plane]. Now they are really wonderful in other areas. They are very unique. In some areas of the teaching they have absolute knowingness that pulls them from this body to about right here [fourth plane]. So with that knowingness, when they focus on something it takes that long for it to manifest [immediately]. So they have evolved their consciousness from way over here [first, second, and third planes] right up to here [upper four planes]. Their mind is developing in this level [fourth plane]. But not all of it is there. A lot of it is still sitting down here [lower planes]. So we have people who can manifest out of thin air an object, but what about telling them to heal themselves? The same person who can manifest out of thin air, you would be impressed and you are going to get to see them. But what if I said to them, "Go over there and heal that person." Suddenly their acceptance moves from this level [fourth plane] down to this level [first plane]. And why do you think that is? Because they accept some things and deny other things. And it is the very things that they accept that they manifest

---

1 See Fig. 22: The Arrow of Time.

straightaway. And it is the very things that they don't accept that they don't get straightaway.

So what about you? The same for you. Today I am going to give you all this knowledge. You are going to know more about the brain than ninety-nine point nine-tenths of the people in your country. And you are going to know about seven bodies that nobody knows about. And you are going to leave here today with the discipline and have manifested three things you want and changed three things you want.

If you have moved yourself up to this utter acceptance, you get them all immediately. Everything starts to fall apart the day you leave here. It is in shambles. Everything falls apart because the glue that holds your present together is the energy and your focus. The moment you change your focus, it is pulled away and all of the energy disperses. Relationships start to change, they fire you from your job, your cat bites you on the leg, your bird flies away, your dog has rabies. Everything falls apart.

Now I want you to expect that. You know why? Because the moment you see things falling into ruins simply means that you have changed your attitude on it, and the moment you change your attitude on it, it pulls it away. Everything crumbles. And if you hold the attitude here, it re-formulates, the same energy. You know, the same energy that makes you sick, you know, if you believe and live a life that is reckless and if you hear the warnings that it is going to be devastating for your health, it always is. But the same energy that caused destruction — it is the same energy; it is not new energy — the same energy that causes destruction can release the destruction the moment the mind releases the focus on it. When the mind changes its mind, the energy falls apart and reconvenes as radiant health, same energy. How many of you understand? So be it.

Now, P.S., runners; I like them. And I do not send them as often as most people would like for me to. But they are my runners that come to teach you something about everything you have learned here. Always bless them, always. If someone is in your face and they are bawling you out, as you call it, and suddenly you realize that what they are saying is true, start laughing and embrace them. They are a runner. Don't slap them and trip them. "What you say is true. Thank you for showing it to me." What does that do for an enemy? If you go around kissing your enemies, you have disarmed them. When you start thanking them for their rudeness, there is no more enemy, is there? How many of you understand? So be it.

Now the teaching we are going to have today — oh, there are other things that I heard, but we will not discuss those — what we are going to learn today I want you to pay very close attention to. And I want you to engage your partner vigorously and I want you to start talking and I want you to get involved with what you are learning. That way the learning will stay with you. And here is something you should know. You can never manifest anything unless you first have the knowledge about it. Got it? How many of you understand? So be it.

CHAPTER SIX
The Auric Field

The Energy Bands
That Surround the Human Body

How many of you have heard the term auric field? Raise your hands. Auric field. Now how many of you believe that you can tear an aura? How many of you believe that? How can you tear energy? How can you rip up a thought? Auras, that is a metaphysical term for a band of energy that is actually dual in nature that surrounds all human beings, and this is what it looks like.[1] Now this energy — Let's say this is you and you have dual bands around the body. In other words, it is not just a gray aura or a blue aura or a rainbow aura. It is very specific about energy because what an aura actually is is levels of frequency with levels of consciousness. Now hold out your arm. Hold out your arm to your side. That is how wide the field is around your body. Now put both of your arms out and stretch them out and look at who all is sitting in your field. So would we say this is a social-conscious group? Indeed we would. Take a look around. Now go sideways. Go sideways and look at who else is in your field.

This field, extending to the tips of your fingers, is actually a set of two bands. The first one ends here

---

1 See Fig. 16: Binary Mind — Living the Image.

217

[the elbow]; the second one ends here [fingertips].[2] It goes all the way around you and it is all the way in front of you and it is moving. The field cannot be seen with human eyes except for that which is termed the field closest to the finger, closest to the hand. If we were to put a black cloth on this wall and set two of you up and the rest of you to the back of the room and turned out the lights except for a small light on, you would be able to see literally the first band in the lower frequency around the body, around everyone that we put in front of that backdrop. You would actually see it. It is not a trick of the light. It is only what is visible to the brain. Got it?

Do you remember yesterday when we were working on this, the seven levels?[3] How many of you remember? Remember we did it first with the hands and then with the drawing? Remember when we started, if you will recall, we talked about the energy between these two points. How many of you remember? And we said that is time. How many of you remember we talked about what happens to this energy if we slow it down to the next level? What happens to it? Turn to your neighbor and tell them what happens to this energy if we bring it down into this time field [sixth level].

Now if we took this energy and slowed it down, it would wind itself up like this.[4] It normally looks like this [a wave], undulating fields called the serpent. If we took then and put all of this nucleus, starting right here, brought it all the way down, we would have what science finds baffling about life. What they find baffling is — they call it subatomic fields — minute particles, atomic particles.

---

2 The first band ends at the level of the elbows; the second band ends at the tips of the fingers when the arms are fully stretched out to the sides.
3 See Fig. 9: Descent of Consciousness and Energy from Point Zero.
4 See Fig. 11: Energy of the Seven Planes of Existence.

FIG. 16: BINARY MIND — LIVING THE IMAGE

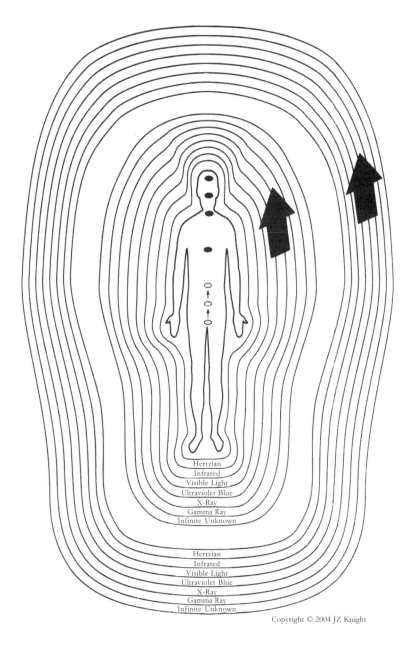

Hertzian
Infrared
Visible Light
Ultraviolet Blue
X-Ray
Gamma Ray
Infinite Unknown

Hertzian
Infrared
Visible Light
Ultraviolet Blue
X-Ray
Gamma Ray
Infinite Unknown

You all know what an atom looks like. If we were to undress an atom, starting with that which is termed its electron and its positrons, if we start to undress it, taking them out first along with that which is termed the outward shield and the momentum there, we could actually undress an atom, starting here [first plane] all the way up to here [seventh plane], and every part would equal one of these levels of time. How many of you understand that?

So science is trying to understand life from the big to the little instead of understanding life from the little to the big. Do you understand? Don't go to sleep. So what this means then, that all matter, including this board and your body, are made up of atoms, that then if you coagulate atoms together in what is called a brotherhood, those atoms create what is called gross matter. Gross matter then creates molecules. Molecules then create tissue. How many of you understand? So be it.

So now if we were to take a microscopic cell out of your body, it would still be big compared to the subatomic field. Are you still with me? Now so what does that tell you, my beautiful students? It says then that all life is made up of condensed consciousness and energy in the form of particles and that what science is endeavoring to understand is how do these partners, how is this partnership formed? How does one atom know to connect and share electrons with another atom? How do they know that? In other words, what is the intelligence behind an atom? For example, if everything that you have on your body is made up of atoms, then why is your garment feeling different than your skin? I am here to tell you that all atoms share a relationship together according to consciousness, and that is the pattern that glues them together.

Remember, energy — energy, like this — energy is

consciousness in motion. It is in motion. So even if we have energy, we have an inextricably riding field called consciousness. So every atom and every part of the atom, all the way to its orbit, has a mind. So every atomic structure has a mind.

Now if we understand that it takes this entire pyramid to create an atom and that it takes time and mind to coagulate that atomic field, we will find out now that we can readily explain on the Earth how everything got here.[5] We had free form of energy. We had a superior intelligence that focused a thought, if you will, a thought-form, if you will, that the thought-form became the lord of energy, and energy mutated and created relationships, coagulated to fill in the pattern of thought. Are you still with me? Every tree, every insect, every grain of sand came from a superior intelligence. And all sand is is coagulated energy in the form of particles, but what holds it together is a mind, and the mind is what has put that atomic field into relationship with itself. It is attracting itself. How many of you understand?

Copyright © 2004 JZ Knight

5 See Fig. 11: Energy of the Seven Planes of Existence.

The Miracles of Yeshua ben Joseph

So then the large is made up of the invisible. The visible is made up of the invisible. So in order to correct the visible, to make change on a geographic scale even in your own reality, it is not about us going and cutting up these things. It is not about us sweeping the sand out of our life. It is about changing our mind to the large structure. Then the large structure falls apart and recoagulates itself into a new relationship to take new form. How many of you understand? You do?

Now so where are these? Where is this fast time? When Yeshua ben Joseph became the Christ, what he was doing was he was living in this time-flow on this scale right here [seventh plane]. His body was made up of all of the particles in this time-flow here [first plane]. Now his consciousness and his mind spent the rest of his life accelerating his mind up this scale, all the way up [seventh plane], so he was able to bring about the mind that flows in this kingdom [seventh plane] and the consciousness that flows in this kingdom [sixth plane]. He was able to take that consciousness into his three-dimensional brain, and so instead of thinking like a three-dimensional person he thought like a sixth-dimensional God. Are you still with me?

Now this kingdom right here [sixth plane] — don't go to sleep — this heaven looks vastly different than this heaven [first plane]. Why, there are lifeforms here that you can't even begin to imagine because you have no reference for it. The only thing you can imagine is what is already set down here [first plane]. The mind that it took to create this kingdom [sixth plane] and its outrageousness and its unlimitedness and its eternalness is the same mind this entity developed down here [first plane]. So look at how he saw life, will you. He knew that however he saw anything is exactly how he agreed for it to be. Are you with me? So when he saw the blind man, when he saw the blind man the blind man asked for help. So he bent over and picked up some clay and he spat in it. And what he was doing with the clay and his spit, he was creating a new biofield of particle relationship. And when he did this and put it together and put it on the blind man's eyes, in molding the clay Yeshua ben Joseph saw perfect vision. So as he was molding the clay, the clay became the catalyst to perfect vision. Are you with me? So when he put the clay on his eyes, that biofield or morphogenic field reconstructed immediately the visual nerve supply to the back of the brain and he saw instantly. Are you with me?

Now we call that a miracle-worker. But how powerful is it to be like this entity, who every day of his life worked up to this level of relationship with the particle field? What did he have to do? Walking down the path he would see — he would choose immediately — whether to agree with the landscape or change it. So if he was walking and stirring up saffron dust, if he found delight in that then he was agreeing with the dust. Are you with me? So the dust never changed, would it? How many times do you walk down the path and stir up dust and are agitated with it? That only enforces its nature, doesn't it? If he walked into a group of people and he is teaching them and then he stops to feed them — listen to me — and he has only a basket of fishes and a loaf of bread and he has five thousand people, what would your mind say? Let's run to the market straightaway; correct? But this was a master who understood the relationship between mind and matter and all he had to do was to change his mind on what he saw. And so the fish and the bread became the seed that multiplied in his mind. And as long as he saw it, the supply was endless. Are you with me? Now where did the supply come from? The supply came from one fish and one loaf of bread, and all he needed to do was to make them multitudinous. So what he did is he kept creating echoes of the fish and the bread, and he was taking energy that was falling apart and recoagulating it, giving them a frame of reference to coagulate into.

If you stop and think about it, someone told the rose to be a rose and someone told it how to smell and someone or something described to the rose in a mental thought deep, velvet red. Someone did that because it didn't just spring up on its own. It was created to be what it is, not only the rose but birds and water and environment. Someone focused them into evolution. Who was that? You, because it is what you expect. How many of you understand?

Now Yeshua ben Joseph was considered a master all the way up to the sixth level. He was only a master; he was never a Christ. And his job, as difficult as it was, was to defy reality with his mind. Look, if I am telling you today that what you think affects all life around you, then if you stop for a moment and reflect, you will see how your life has stayed static according to your image thoughts. You drive down the city, you expect to see the city, the city is there. You expect to see people begging, they are always there. You expect to see a car wreck on the side of the road because you need a little excitement, there is always one, isn't there? If that is true and you have the power, imagine what an initiation it was for such a being, and beings, that every day they had to defy physical reality and overlay with a mind so powerful that they could see what was not there and make it that. Powerful, eh?

Do you think that that is more powerful than you? No, it is you. But where is your energy? Your energy is that you accept what is mundane in your life. You accept your ill health, you accept your problems, you accept your limitations, and because you accept them you freeze them and lock then that energy into a relationship. That is what you do every day. You are a God. You are doing that. Imagine what it would be to get up every morning and defy reality, to start changing what has been normal to you to be supernormal every day. So the first day you get up and a few things change but not everything. Is that enough to go back and accept mundane reality? Or is it that we are having to create a mind that is so powerful that it can acquiesce the energy field of any lifeform and any situation and change it immediately. What does that take? Constant focus on what is expected rather than what is seen.

The Observer Effect in Quantum Mechanics

The study of quantum mechanics — quanta, meaning packets of energy, the mechanical activity of energy — is a noble science, and it is gaining a stronghold now back into that which is termed the scientific community. And what is different in quantum mechanics than in, let us say, Sir Isaac Newton's field of reality is that quantum mechanics says, like the scientist's experience, that whatever you think a particle is going to be like, it always is — always is. So they began to understand then that particle behavior had absolutely everything to do with the Observer.

So imagine a scientist — imagine this for a moment — is going to set up an experiment with light.[6] And he draws a board and he draws a little slit. Let me show you what this is, very comical. He is going to shoot light photons through to a board. This is the board; it is a negative. But here is an obstruction; here is a wall. And he has got his little photon machine right here. Well, what he has done is he made a little tiny slit right here. So if he shoots the light out, it should go in a straight direction. And what he wants to see, that if light makes it through this barrier it will show up as little dots on the negative on this wall here. So he turns the machine on and he shoots the ray of light out, and guess what the light does? It sneaks right down here, comes right in, and hits the wall. Well, that was pretty amazing. He said, "That light had a mind of its own. How did it know to do that?" Then he said, "Well, we will take care of this." So he plugs up the hole so now it can't get through. So he turns the light on and it just makes light bombardment onto this wall.

So then he does another experiment. He gives it two options. So he makes a little slit here and a wee little slit down here, turns it on again, and half go through this slit and half go through that slit. "Well, I'll be. How did it know to do that?" How did it know to do that? Who is the Observer observing light particles? Who is it? (Audience: The scientist.)

6 In 1803 Thomas Young used the double-slit experiment to show that light was a wave in nature. Subsequently, Albert Einstein, following the studies of Max Planck, concluded that light was a composition of particles called photons. Nevertheless, Albert Einstein could not deny the results from Young's experiment. The discoveries of these two scientists gave rise to the problem of the wave-particle duality. That is the problem of whether light is a wave or a particle. In 1924, Niels Bohr, H. A. Kramers, and John Slater suggested that the wave-particle duality could be solved if the waves in question were probability waves. Probability waves show the probable location of a particle collapsing at any given time. Finally, the development and application of the theories of quantum

Louder. That is it. So what did he have in mind to do with the light? Wasn't he going to test it? But in his mind did he give a little way in which it could get through? Did he? Well, then if he did that, then his mind is exactly what the light is going to do. The light knows to go through the slit because the scientist knows it is there. Have you got it? How many are with me?

FIG. 17: THE DOUBLE-SLIT EXPERIMENT

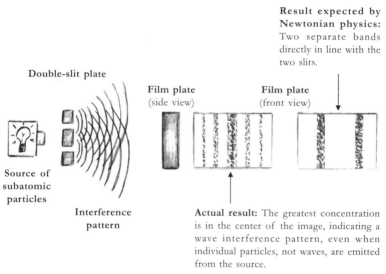

Result expected by Newtonian physics: Two separate bands directly in line with the two slits.

Double-slit plate

Film plate (side view)

Film plate (front view)

Source of subatomic particles

Interference pattern

Actual result: The greatest concentration is in the center of the image, indicating a wave interference pattern, even when individual particles, not waves, are emitted from the source.

---

mechanics in the research studies of Erwin Schrödinger and Werner Heisenberg were able to correctly predict the location and the characteristic energy levels of an atom. The most important implication arising from the study of quantum mechanics is the role that the Observer plays in the nature of reality. David Bohm, in his book *Wholeness and the Implicate Order* (London: Routledge, 1980), p. 134, concludes that "Rather, the primary emphasis is now on undivided wholeness, in which the observing instrument is not separable from what is observed." Some modern quantum physicists are taking seriously the role of the Observer by exploring the relationship and role of consciousness in the material world. See Amit Goswami, *The Self-Aware Universe* (New York: Tarcher/Putnam, 1995).

Now so science calls this the Observer effect so much to the point that they begin to understand something else, which is important in understanding this [Point Zero] and this [mirror consciousness], that inasmuch as they have always concluded that, for example, a hydrogen atom with its electron, they have always concluded that these electrons that are in orbit around are there in orbit, because when they study them they see them at different trajectories around the nuclei. But when they came to the realization that the Observer is always affecting particles, then they came to the conclusion that there was no particle orbiting the atom but rather it was an electron cloud. In other words, it was just a cloud moving like this. And they were correct. And do you know when they discovered the electron? When they expected to find it there. You like that?

So imagine what all these atoms are doing when we turn our backs. Imagine a pool table. You turn around and all of the balls are there. You turn your back and they fuzz out. The moment you turn around and look at them, they are back to normal. That is the way that it is. How do you know the Earth is still around when you go to bed at night? How do you know you are here? And this is a great leap for science because if that is correct, they have to make the next step and they have to say you are creating life. Now do they dare say that? Why, they will be burned at the stake, put up in front of a firing squad because that is heresy. But it is truth. So now if that is so, then the mind of the most humble man or woman is constantly holding form. And don't you know what a law is? A law says you have to obey the form and to break it is against the law. You are operating on a law of an agreement. You agree that this is the way that it is. How many of you understand? Now if you are affecting the fields out there, then with what?

When Yeshua ben Joseph was moving his mind up to this lofty state and held it there, he was actually not of this world but indeed, as it has been said, he was in the world. His spiritual self was coming from here [sixth plane] while his physical remained here [first plane]. And it wasn't until he got to here [sixth plane] that he had to die. This is the ultimate test, that he had to agree to die as the final initiation. What a final test. How do you defy death? First off, you have to die; otherwise it isn't a test, is it?

Now imagine how terrifying that is. None of you are at that place yet. But imagine what it would be to fully develop God on this plane. How would he do that? His final test would be that he would agree to die in front of everyone, and that so powerful was his mind, in which he called "the Father within me," within him — the Father within him was this entity right here [Point Zero] that we all have — so powerful was he that he allowed the body to die and to go into decay. And then at the appropriate moment he was to reestablish a relationship with the body. Is that possible? Students, is that possible? Given what scientists say that we do with particles, is that possible? It is indeed.

So where is the loophole here? The loophole is that we are so terrified of life that we never live. We are so terrified of dying that we never live life. No one in this room has the capacity to do that because no one has built up such a wall of reality that "lay the body dead as it is, I will resurrect it." No one has developed that yet because they haven't lived yet. So imagine what kind of body that he had then. The body went into physical corruption within three days, and he came back. What was it that came back? Well, you see this drawing that we did here?[7] When I told you yesterday that we were descending into involution to this time, that is

---

7 See Fig. 9: Descent of Consciousness and Energy from Point Zero.

true, we have. We all have echo, meaning we have contributed to the atmosphere as well as the mind on every one of these levels, so we have a body already existing on every one of these time frames, already there. It is already there. Hard to believe, isn't it? But we have a body here in the physical form. We have a body here, here, here, here, here, and here [all seven levels]. The body that we left behind is an echo. It is a mind. It is rolled up. It is rolled up waiting to be unrolled, just like this little entity here is rolled up.[8]

The moment we access any one of these bodies, we do so by focusing — equal to our level of acceptance, equal to one of these levels — and when we do we start to unroll the atmosphere in that level and that becomes the stream of consciousness that moves into the brain through the back of the brain called the reptilian. It is a stream of mind, moves right in here and activates the neocortices. And this is so familiar, this place is so familiar when it is accessed, you will wonder how come you left it behind. But the moment that you leave it, you will think it is a dream because it has rolled back up into this atmosphere here.

FIG. 18: SEVEN BODIES ENFOLDED WITHIN EACH OTHER

8 See Fig. 9: Descent of Consciousness and Energy from Point Zero.

So every human being has seven bodies and they are enfolded in this body [physical body], and they radiate into what is called the auric field that extends to the tips of your fingers. All seven bodies are enfolded inside of the gross matter that makes up the physical incarnation you have now. If you have been living on this timeline for ten and a half million years and at 455,000 years here we had an abrupt change to this [the brain] — we only developed that about 40,000 years ago — so all of the bodies have been on a wheel of incarnation in which the wheel never got any further than the third level. Now what does that mean? That means then that on every lifetime we had completely contained within us at any one time four radiant bodies. On death we are in the third body, and enfolded in the lightbody are four other bodies, four other frequencies. Going to the light is not the end of the story. It is only a familiar place. But enfolded inside the light/radiant body are yet four other bodies that access different levels of time. They are our vehicle to get there. How many of you understand?

Christ's Resurrection and Seven Levels of Consciousness

Now, today, your last lifetime you never went any further than the light. At the light, before you came back to this incarnation, you reviewed your last life. The review took place in your lightbody. It reviewed, unfolded all of the energy, and gave you a living screen to see what you did, who you were, what you accomplished, how you evolved, where you didn't evolve. It just unrolled the energy and allowed it to play. Then once you had decided or made up your mind to come back, you were thinking with a lightbody, not a human body, but you were still cognizant that you could have done better in the physical body. Don't you find it interesting that entities who go to the light talk about viewing their life and that they viewed it with a cognitive judgment? They didn't have a brain. How were they able to make an opinion of what they saw? Because they did have a brain. What was the brain? It wasn't the gray tissue that is sitting up here but it was a brain equal to the body they were inhabiting.

When you die, you move immediately into infrared. It is the psychic realm. From the psychic realm the shaft of light appears and you go down it and you are actually moving from low infrared to the high end of infrared. Then you hit the light. Who is the light? You. It is there that you view everything. While you are making a decision about your physical life, there are four other potential lives or bodies that are enfolded in the light. And all you keep doing is agreeing to come back to this one. How many of you understand? So you have never changed — never changed — those four other bodies [upper seals]. They are what we call hidden.

We always change the lightbody because the lightbody looks just like the body you are sitting in today, except younger and healthier. Why does it look like the body you have today? Because the body you have today couldn't look the way it looked unless it had a light-field around it to give it the mind to be that way. How many of you understand? So we are always recycling the lightbody, the infrared body, and the physical body, but we have yet to use the hidden bodies of the upper four realms.

Now stay with me. Don't go to sleep. I am going to give you a lot of knowledge. Don't be bored.

All of these bodies are in you and around you. If you look at your hand and you think about the atomic field that we just discussed earlier — think about this — then the radiating field off of one singular atom is equal to the radiating field of one of those bodies. In other words, every atom in your hand is the composite of seven levels of time. You got it? So the hand is a product of seven levels condensed to this [physical matter]. But what if we could defy that reality? What if we defied our body looking this way and insisted on it looking another way? Would it be possible to do that? How many of you agree? Absolutely is. You see, quantum mechanics doesn't say this works for the electrons but not for you. This field that surrounds your body has got within it the seven bodies hidden within your own tissue. When this dies, it gives up one body in the beginning. The one body is infrared. But in the infrared body are contained all the other higher bodies and you keep peeling them off. Do you understand?

Now so what does this, this, this, and this [the upper four bodies] have to do with Yeshua ben Joseph becoming a Christ? Because he had to prove that he was accessing the upper kingdom of God. And he had proved it every single way by all of the miracles and the teachings that he imparted. But there was one thing that terrified all men in their hearts and that was death. You see, the Hellenistic Jews of that time were the only ones that believed in reincarnation. The Jews of Abraham did not believe in reincarnation. They believed in hell, which was the most terrifying aspect, and that simply meant a shallow grave, that they would be dismembered.

Yeshua ben Joseph had to show to a culture of people that there was life after death. And the way that he had to do that is he had to sacrifice his own life. So he has to pull out this consciousness right here [first seal], this one right here [second seal]. And he has to let the body die and he has to move all the way, unfolding all of those bodies all the way until he is right here [seventh seal], and he says, "My Father and I are one." He is saying that "My mind is no longer from the House of David in these terrible times. My mind is my Father within me," who is this mind, the first mind. And he had to take off every one of those bodies, even the lightbody. He couldn't keep it on. He had to pull off the lightbody, manifest the Blue Body®. He had to pull off the Blue Body®, which is Shiva, and manifest the golden body. He had to pull off the golden body, go to the rose body, and then he had to go to Infinite Unknown, which he went here. And only until he did that was he incorruptible.

And it was from this state right here [seventh plane] that he resurrected this body down here and gave it life, but what he gave it is eternal life. In other words, his body down here was vibrating nearly at the rate of light. And he only kept it slow so that he could interact with people and give them the last teaching. And why was his body radiating so fast? Because that was where his consciousness was. God now was man. And he lifted it up and reconstructed its physical matter, but he reconstructed it from the point of God, so it was vibrating very fast. So when he left, where did he go? He simply raised, kept raising, the frequency. In other words, he started this spin around this atom, and then the spin collapsed inward to the inside of the nucleus and it started spinning. And all the time, all the time he was doing that, all of that spin allowed every one of those particles to go into free space. So he was unfolding the seven bodies. And when he disappeared, he disappeared at light.

Now that was only when he was called the Christ, the arisen one. That was the last test. That meant his consciousness had to be one with this so absolutely that not even death could defy that mind. And doing so, we now have great myth and legend and religion circling this entity. But what has never been told to you: It is not that Jesus is going to save your life but rather that he was a master who demonstrated the power of God in man and that if anyone had the eyes to see it, then they would understand. And if anyone had the ears to hear the message, they were offered the message, and they had to be simple enough to understand the transmutation of the human Spirit into eternity, and it was demonstrated. And it wasn't demonstrated just with him. It has been demonstrated throughout the eons in every culture because people soon forget.

So what do we have now? We have now a religion around Jesus being the only son of God. That doesn't make any sense because everyone is the sons and daughters of God, not just him. And he can't save you. If he did, he would have done so in the first century. You understand? But his message is this. And how come he didn't teach his disciples this? Because they were simple men. They were fishermen. They were tax collectors. They were people just like you. How could he teach them that? He couldn't. All he could do was to teach them in parables and in deeds. And he said, "Believe. If your eye lies to you, pluck it out. If you believe and your arm defies you, cut it off." That was an analogy to say no matter what your physical body does, it isn't the truth. Understand?

CHAPTER SEVEN
Kundalini Energy and the Seven Seals

The Seven Seals

Now in every one of you, you have this same triad, and the power that is around your body is enfolded not only around your body but in your body.[1] The human body with its brain and its seven centers — these are not chakras — these are called seals. A chakra is where two lines of energy cross, and that is a chakra point. These are called seven seals. Every one of you has it. They are equal to this pyramid right here. And how simple is this? It means that what is important to you is where your energy will sit. And how many of you in this audience, that the only thing important to you is your sexuality, which is here, procreation [first seal], your pain and suffering, which is right here [second seal]. That is all that is important to you. You like to suffer and make other people suffer. You are warlike creatures. Or you are powerful people. You are tyrants. You are tyrants and you are victims [third seal]. These attitudes have to do with these vortexes right here [first three seals]. They are called seals.

And everyone in this room has these open. What does this mean? It means that the first three bodies' energies are working on this level here, this three-dimensional Earth plane with its time-flow, because it is necessary to have these open in order to exist down here. But these also are delivering

1 See Figs. 9 and 19.

energy every day. So whatever you think, the energy in your body opens. So just imagine this: Yeshua ben Joseph was born from the first seal. He grew up going through his youth and having this center activated [first seal], having this center activated [second seal], and having — at his last test in the desert of forty days, his Boktau — his power being tested through abuse right here [third seal]. Now that is as far as anyone goes on this plane. That is not to demean intelligence. We can have a neocortex-brilliant person, but their energy is only here [first seal]. Neocortex brilliance usually is in agreement with the establishment, so this energy is open here [first three seals].

Let's think about Yeshua ben Joseph. In order for him to have healed the blind man, he had to have had energy not coming out of here [first three seals] but that energy had to have come from there [upper four seals]. He had to open up and develop and make manifest his fifth-level mind, the mind that exists up here, in order for him to perform a miracle down here. So what did that mean? That meant that that moment all of his energy was sitting here [higher seals], not down here [first three seals].

Your body today has seven seals just like this. And you have a drawing; take it out.[2] This drawing here is the way that this physical body is held together according to these doors right here [first three seals]. So in every human being we have energy spiraling out of this center [first seal], we have energy spiraling out of this center [second seal] and this center [third seal]. Now if that is what is pulsating out here, if this is the energy that is manifesting as sexuality, power, or pain — stretch your arms out again — how many people do you affect with that attitude? Turn sideways. Have I made my point? So be it. Now if we could take and unlock

2 See Fig. 19: The Seven Seals: Seven Levels of Consciousness in the Human Body.

FIG. 19: THE SEVEN SEALS:
SEVEN LEVELS OF CONSCIOUSNESS IN THE HUMAN BODY

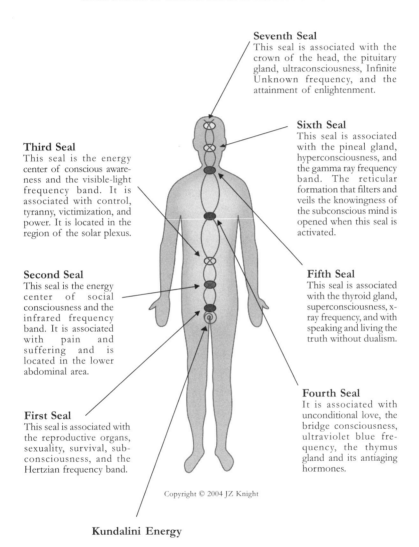

Seventh Seal
This seal is associated with the crown of the head, the pituitary gland, ultraconsciousness, Infinite Unknown frequency, and the attainment of enlightenment.

Sixth Seal
This seal is associated with the pineal gland, hyperconsciousness, and the gamma ray frequency band. The reticular formation that filters and veils the knowingness of the subconscious mind is opened when this seal is activated.

Third Seal
This seal is the energy center of conscious awareness and the visible-light frequency band. It is associated with control, tyranny, victimization, and power. It is located in the region of the solar plexus.

Second Seal
This seal is the energy center of social consciousness and the infrared frequency band. It is associated with pain and suffering and is located in the lower abdominal area.

Fifth Seal
This seal is associated with the thyroid gland, superconsciousness, x-ray frequency, and with speaking and living the truth without dualism.

First Seal
This seal is associated with the reproductive organs, sexuality, survival, sub-consciousness, and the Hertzian frequency band.

Fourth Seal
It is associated with unconditional love, the bridge consciousness, ultraviolet blue frequency, the thymus gland and its antiaging hormones.

Kundalini Energy

241

these [higher seals], then we would unlock these [upper four frequency bands] and we would activate these [upper four levels of consciousness]. If we did, we could then change all reality and bring about a lofty mind to re-create it.

Now I want you to take out the drawing of this picture here that shows the seven seals in the body.[3] I want you to put it in front of you. I want you to take and put your right hand, position it on your body where it is indicated on the drawing, and then I want you to read steadfastly the description of each one of those seals, touching your body in that part, making contact with it. You may begin straightaway.

Kundalini Energy

Now I want you to take a red color, the color red, and I want you to draw what looks like a sleeping serpent right underneath the first seal — a sleeping serpent, the color red — a coiled, sleeping serpent.

How many of you have heard of the term kundalini, the kundalini? The kundalini is an old term that in ancient law says that in every human being there lies the sleeping serpent or the sleeping dragon and that it is the dragon or serpent energy of life, and it lies coiled at the base of the spine. Ancient teachings also say that when this serpent is aroused, some very extraordinary things happen, that this energy is not the same energy that is responsible for the energy coming out of the first, second, and third seals. This is sort of like a large packet of quanta. It is something that is reserved for something very special that is hidden, reserved for human evolution. It is said that when the

---

3 See Fig. 19: The Seven Seals: Seven Levels of Consciousness in the Human Body.

serpent arises, it splits itself. And if we draw that which is termed a spine, the skull, that this serpent sitting at the base of the spine — Understand the spine is also that which is termed the spinal column that allows electrical information from all the nervous systems to be supplied to the entire body, so this spine and this energy is particularly interested in this particular path. This path, from the base of the spine to the front of what is called the silent place, the front of the neocortices, that is called the journey, and it is the journey of enlightenment. When this serpent wakes up, it splits and starts to dance around the spine. And what it is, it is powerful energy that as it is moving up and down the spinal column, utilizing that which is termed spinal liquid in this form here down this pathway, it is actually ionizing spinal fluid and changing its molecular structure. So as this serpent dances up the spine here, it is changing that which is termed the basic DNA pattern of the entire body. Moreover, the end of its journey means that the serpent's energy moves up into this aspect of the brain right here [lower cerebellum].

The reptilian brain surrounds the upper brainstem in an area called the reticular formation. I want you to take a look at this on your drawing right here.[4] It looks like a mesh of webs, right here. Now listen to me very carefully. The seat of the subconscious is not in the midbrain; it is in the reptilian brain. The subconscious is located here [lower cerebellum]. Moreover, this reticular formation, as you have seen on your drawing, is actually a trunk line of switches that allows certain information to go and to flow onto the neocortex up here. This is a computer. Whatever is programmed into it becomes reality, especially affecting the body. So when the serpent energy or the dragon energy of

4 See Fig. 21: The Brain.

the kundalini rises up the spinal column, it is ionizing with polarized energy this entire fluid that flows up and down the spinal column. When it hits the reticular formation, it opens up all of the switches. Now what does that mean? All of the doors to the subconscious are flung open. Further, the energy, like a dynamic conqueror marching, destroying, setting on fire everything in its path, is the march of the kundalini.

When it comes to what is called the midbrain section, this entity here called the thalamus in ancient terms was called the guardian at the door. And in myth and lore everyone thinks that the guardian at the door is Saint Peter, but it is not so. It is Saint Thalamus. The kundalini energy activates this door to be open. Now the thalamus is critical in the midbrain section because it also is the protector of the pineal gland, and you are going to learn a little bit more about that later. But the thalamus is where all the trunk lines from that which is termed the nerve endings meet and all of the fibers from the reticular formation meet, and it is a switching point. When the kundalini opens this energy, what it means in effect is that everything that has been hidden from you in the form of the subconscious, now that energy flows free will to a specific point in the brain, this area right here, the frontal lobe. Why is that so dramatic? Because the kundalini opening up the switches and doorways, allowing ancient knowledge to come to the surface, it really is allowing the subconscious total access to your conscious mind.

We call the kundalini a tribute to total enlightenment, because total enlightenment means when you get to peer beyond the veil you get to know what has never been known. You get to experience in a moment all that there is and in a moment you know all that there is. In a flash of blinding light you can immediately see all the lives that you have lived and all the ones you are going to live, and immediately it is all known. How is that possible? The kundalini energy, or the dragon force of the Near East, sits here [base of the spine], has been encoded. It was set there to be, as we would call it, rocket fuel to enlightenment. This energy, how do I describe it in terms of the triad? Which one of these energies is it? Which one of these is it? It is none of them. The kundalini is — Let's do this. Remember when I took you from this point here [Point Zero] where you were created by the Void and then you contemplated yourself and created the first level? You remember? Well, remember we went all the way down, we are falling all the way down to way out here — we are down here on the first plane, three-dimensional; that is where you are right now — and that I said to you that the consciousness that operates the human brain swings like a pendulum. It is supposed to, in order to dream.

There is a magic moment that happens that even science now recognizes, that in the swinging of a pendulum, just as the swinging of human consciousness, there is a moment that it pauses. Come on, let's go way out here.[5] Let's swing like a pendulum for a moment: negative/positive, no/yes, lower/higher, dark/light. Now let's do it in slow motion. Is there a moment when the movement of this hand is not going forward or not going backwards? Is there a moment when it is standing still? How many of you agree? There is. It is the moment it comes right up in alignment with this hand here.[6] When you put both levels of consciousness in alignment like this, we call this the eternal Now — the eternal Now. It is the center of the magnet. At this moment here there is a dynamic force of energy that is

5 See Fig. 12: Dreaming the Dream.
6 See Fig. 13: The Now Alignment.

reflected from this mirror to this God. It is like in a tunnel, right here. That tunnel energy is exactly what the kundalini is. Now it is rarely ever shaken from its slumber in human consciousness because most human beings have this shut down and they are doing this [swinging].[7] Understand? In other words, to totally know, to totally be focused, to totally be unaware that you are human is a very rare moment indeed. That only comes when we have two levels of consciousness working, the Observer and the doer. Got it? Now if we wake this [kundalini energy] back up and we put this into focus of it, the force-field between these two [points of consciousness] is like a powerful magnet. You understand?

Now I am telling you this very simple and very childlike. Whenever you dream a dream, it means that your consciousness has moved out here [forward swing]. It is dreaming. It is dreaming. When it is finished with the dream, it is supposed to move like this [alignment]. In other words, it is a mirror. It has captured the drawing; correct?[8] Its natural momentum is to close up like this. The pyramid is collapsing to Point Zero. That means that in order to affect reality we have to take a drawing back to God so it closes up all time and we are in a no-place. We disappear for a moment. When these part, look what happens. We have closed up the pyramid. Now we are pulling this vacuum, this energy, back down. What is important about this pull? What is important about it is that our dream was the new program for energy and we are pulling the energy down with a mental thought. So every one of our bodies, every atom in our body, is reshuffled and reprogrammed according to this dream. Got it?

---

7 See Fig. 14: The Swing Movement of the Mirror Consciousness.
8 The drawing of the dream we want to focus on and manifest.

So we are naturally supposed to dream, focus just like this, into a Now. Nothing else exists except this [the Now]. When this is accomplished, it is this energy that is moving up the body that is bringing about the state of euphoria. This euphoric state is when the dragon awakens, when these are in alignment to one another. Close it up, bring it back, it is destiny. Bring it all the way back, move off,[9] the serpent has now programmed the entire cellular structure and is now collapsing back into form all the way down here [first plane]. Move off of it and the next moment reality is re-formed. That is how it works. Turn to your neighbor and explain it briefly, what is the kundalini. Do you understand? How many of you understand philosophically about the kundalini? It is an energy that exists only in total alignment in the Now. That is the only time that energy exists.

Now how many of you recognize this drawing?[10] What is it? Caduceus. What does this symbol represent? Health. What does this look like to you? Well, the staff looks like the spinal column. The orb on top is representative of the brain. The two different serpents winding in complement to one another and then facing the orb look like the kundalini, doesn't it? And why do we have wings on the orb? What would the wings represent symbolically? Freedom. It is no accident that the caduceus, representing absolute health and well-being, is represented in the medical profession, except they forgot what it means, because this sign of antiquity tells us that when we move into the Now with the focus of radiant health, and if we can hold the Now, this is exactly the story of what happens and we are healed.

---

9 See Fig. 14: The Swing Movement of the Mirror Consciousness.
10 See Fig. 20: The Caduceus.

FIG. 20: THE CADUCEUS

The only way we are healed is if we can raise this energy to start circling our spinal column, moving all the way up to our head and in its journey ionizing the magnetic field that it is creating. It is changing the nucleonic spin of all the atoms that make up our body and is reshuffling the DNA. So how many of you have heard of people who healed themselves with their minds? That tells you how they did it.

The Brain

Now take out your drawing on the brain and out loud to yourself, as I point, I want you to read the names and associate yourself with this area of the brain. Look at your drawing and look at it. (Audience: Reptilian brain.) Louder. Or lower cerebellum. Louder. Now let's pause here for a moment. It was once thought that the pineal gland was the seat of the soul. It is not the seat of the soul. Let's continue. (Audience: Midbrain, corpus callosum, neocortex, thalamus.) Saint Thalamus. Look at your drawing. If you want to call this a hippopotamus, you can. It is all right with me. It is the hippocampus, amygdala.

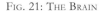

FIG. 21: THE BRAIN

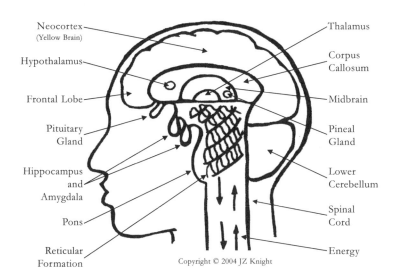

Neocortex
(Yellow Brain)

Hypothalamus

Frontal Lobe

Pituitary
Gland

Hippocampus
and
Amygdala

Pons

Reticular
Formation

Thalamus

Corpus
Callosum

Midbrain

Pineal
Gland

Lower
Cerebellum

Spinal
Cord

Energy

Copyright © 2004 JZ Knight

This is the original two-dimensional caricature-style drawing Ramtha used for his teaching on the function of the brain and its processes. He explained that the different aspects of the brain in this particular drawing are exaggerated and colorfully highlighted for the sake of study and understanding. This specific drawing became the standard tool used in all the subsequent teachings on the brain.

Now let's take a look at the brain now that you have familiarized yourself and mapped yourself with its parts.[11] Let us do this. This is a timeline. Just draw underneath this drawing a timeline. And you can start here with number one. That is the first day you found yourself here [first plane]. Let's go on down to about here, and I want you to date this line 455,000 years ago, 455- years ago. And I want you to come down here a little bit further and I want you to make another line right here, and I want you to date it 40,000, another one right after it 35,000, and then barely in front of that — what is your year as you call it? — and put that timeline there: day one, 455,000 years, 40,000 years, 35,000 years, and today. Now underneath the timeline up to this point I want you to write ten and one-half million years. Now right up to 455,000 years, now we are talking about time as an arrow. It is linear. So now let's turn and look back on the arrow where it came from, from whence it came.[12]

FIG. 22: THE ARROW OF TIME

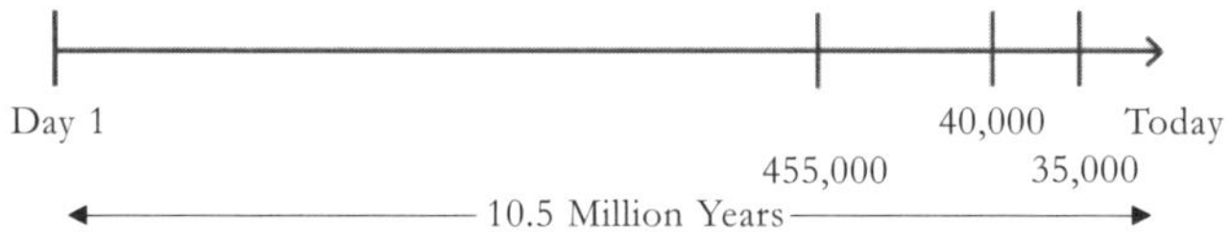

Day 1   40,000   Today
                                          455,000   35,000
        ◄————————— 10.5 Million Years —————————►

---

11 See Fig. 21: The Brain. See also Michelangelo's painting, *The Creation of Adam*, in the Sistine Chapel at the Vatican. Ramtha explained that Michelangelo understood the function of the brain in the creation of reality. This famous painting portrays God reaching out to man from the frontal lobe of the brain. The blue-green cloak below God and the angels represents the spinal cord and helps to identify the brain in this painting.
12 See Fig. 22: The Arrow of Time.

If we look in this time area here [prior to 455,000 years], this human brain looked drastically different. We did not have that which is termed the amygdala. We had the hippocampus. We did not have the frontal lobe, as we know it, or the neocortex. Prior to 455,000 years, let's take a look at how large the brain was. It was only this large. How many of you have seen the skulls of hominids of antiquity? Now imagine for a moment, remember how small the back of the skull was? Do you remember? The back of the skull ended where the corpus callosum is, so all it had was this. That was prior to 455,000 years. Now that is not a bad thing since this was the original brain. Now it is called the reptilian brain because they dated it to that which is termed the reptilian era, and it has been around at least that long. But do not confuse that this is the brain of a reptile, although some people, it could be argued, they have acted like that.

Now if this is the brainstem coming up — Let's use our arm as an example.[13] Make a fist up here, and this will be the midbrain section, this is the brainstem, and right in here is the reticular formation. Now take this other hand, wrap it very tightly around your wrist. The reptilian brain, or the lower cerebellum, has a very tight grip on the spinal column. In other words, all information coming from the brain to the body, all information coming from the body to the brain, is edited by this brain here [lower cerebellum]. Now have you got a grip? This fabulous hominid brain was much more spectacular than we have given it credit for. The human being itself looked vastly different than what you look today, especially in the cranium and the lower cranium. But this brain has been around since the beginning.

---

13 Ramtha uses his arm in the vertical position, with the hand closed, as an example of the brainstem and the midbrain section.

We are carrying it with us through evolution. But this was the brain that we accessed all levels of energy with when we were first in this body. The tissue of this brain is vastly different than the neocortex. Let us say we took a shave. We took a little razor and we took a little tiny shave of the material of this organ and we put it under a microscope. That tiny shaving of the lower cerebellum has more tissue, more atoms in one slice, than the entire neocortex put together.

So this grainy, darkly colored organ is the transmitter and receiver from all of these levels here [all seven levels]. So the first hominid was actually us, bringing with us the intelligence of that which is termed six other bodies, and we unfolded a stream of consciousness through this mechanism here. The yellow brain, the neocortices, does not receive a stream of consciousness. That stream of consciousness only enters here [lower cerebellum] and it enters at the back of the brain here. So we get new knowledge from the back door, not up here [neocortex].

This reptilian brain then became — up to 455,000 years ago — it was our transmitter and receiver to the higher and multiplex dimensions of which we had just come from. The midbrain section was intact, and that which is called the pineal gland was much larger prior to 455,000 years than it is today. And the reason is if the reptilian brain is the seat of the subconscious, the midbrain itself is the seat of all psychic activity. It was created to be that way. The midbrain section is sensitive as a receiver to infrared radiation. Now it is the only part of the brain that is sensitive to infrared radiation. In other words, infrared would be if you are occupying this level at eight hertz, the second level up from this, which happens the moment you die; you enter that realm. That is called the infrared realm. Now infrared as a band has a low end and a high end of its wavelength. This is what we have called the second plane of reality, very far from where we came. This band, because its wave is faster than out here, is called the psychic realm. The hominids prior to 455,000 years ago were telepathic. They communed much like the animals do today. Animals today are very telepathic creatures. Their brains are ultrasensitive to infrared radiation, and infrared is the psychic band.

So the hominids picked up and received thought through the bandwidths, and their brain was the perfect receiver. They picked up communication with this area right in here. The pineal gland, often called the soul of man, it is called that because it is the pineal gland that is responsible for manufacturing two neurotransmitters that are tantamount to consciousness in the yellow brain. The neurotransmitter serotonin — don't go to sleep — we call her Sara for short. Sara is a day girl. The pineal gland, when there is light, is producing serotonin. Think of serotonin as a key. Now the moment the light diminishes in the retina of the eye that contains the same cells — your eye in its retina contains the same cells that are located in the pineal gland — so the moment that light begins to darken, it signals the pineal gland then to stop manufacturing Sara and start manufacturing Mel. Melatonin is the second neurotransmitter and melatonin is created to put the body to sleep.

So they configured that the off- and on-switch of human behavior was located in the head, and when they finally realized that it was the pineal gland they said, ah, that is the master switch. It is not.

However, it is the gland that we call the gland of the sixth seal, is tantamount, important because — listen to me very carefully — if this little gland, according to your eye, as soon as light penetrates your eyelid — that is why your eyelids are transparent, so even if they are closed you still get light in when the light comes up — the moment light starts to hit the retina, this starts to produce the serotonin.

Serotonin is the get-up-and-get-going neurotransmitter. It unlocks everybody that is asleep and turns them on. Now the moment the light diminishes, is seen through here, it switches and produces melatonin. It is the thing that makes you lazy and lethargic and puts you to sleep. However, if the pineal gland is a little factory that manufactures these very important neurotransmitters, it does something else extraordinary: It synthesizes from melatonin a hallucinogenic drug called pinoline. Would you write that down, pinoline.

The pineal gland synthesizes from melatonin a hallucinogenic drug called pinoline.

I do not spell. Pinoline. How does it sound? It sounds like a hallucinogenic.

Now the shaman in the brain is the pineal gland. After midnight, at around one in the morning until about three in the morning, you move into your deepest level of sleep and your most lucid dreams occur there. Lucid dreaming is only possible if the pineal gland has had enough time to take Mel and change Mel into pinoline. And why pinoline? Pinoline is the hallucinogenic that the subconscious uses to allow the brain to communicate with the deeper spheres. You got that? Now people who stay up late at night don't get to produce pinoline and therefore are robbed of this communication. What that means is that pinoline, distributed throughout the sleeping neocortex, fire-reverses the neurons, thereby allowing this entity [mirror consciousness] to talk to this entity [Point Zero]. Got it? Pinoline opens the door to the subconscious mind and, if it does, it allows out-of-body experiences to occur. Furthermore, it allows prophetic vision to be seen on the timeline. And it allows you to move up into these [higher] layers of consciousness, and that before you return to your body, the pinoline that is a short burst in the neocortex is absorbed, and that is all that is produced, and the door shuts and you are back in your body. Got it? How many of you understand? Now the pineal gland produces what? Louder. And how about after midnight? Is there truth to the Cinderella story?

Now when the kundalini rises and hits this area [pineal gland], it immediately — immediately, by virtue of its alignment and its energy — ionizes the spin ratio in the neurotransmitter serotonin.

Now when we say ionizing the spin, what does that mean? Fancy words, eh? Well, if serotonin is a neurotransmitter molecule, then all molecules are made up of atoms. How many of you agree? Correct? Now the atoms that it takes to make a molecule of serotonin is that they have all agreed to have an association and in that association their spins are relative to one another. They interchange electrons together, thereby changing mass, which in turn changes its chemical nature. So if this is a molecule of serotonin, and then we have a hot wind of kundalini and we have a powerful magnetic field of kundalini passing through this molecule, that energy is going to reverse-spin that molecule, thereby changing its characteristic. The molecule itself becomes fractured and then is reconfigured, and what it is reconfigured in is its highest body — never its lower body — its highest body. The highest molecule potential of serotonin is pinoline.

So then this energy moves up into the midbrain, opens the door of Saint Thalamus. Energy moves and starts firing simultaneously on the left and right hemispheres of the brain. All of the neurons start to fire. And with pinoline, immaculately changed in the twinkling of an eye, the brain is thereby capable of logging and registering timelines that go back to a point of eternity. Now turn to your neighbor and explain what I have just taught you about the brain so far. Now, my beautiful people, you have a little better understanding about what is sitting between your ears?

What is this? The pituitary gland is the seventh seal, it is the crown, because the pituitary gland directly affects the yellow brain and is the turn-on of all other glands starting from in the head throughout the rest of the body. The pituitary gland does this by secreting certain hormones that then in turn turn on the pineal. The pineal then secretes its hormones and its neurotransmitters and turns on all of the rest of the glands going down into the body. If you were to have this removed, this entity right here [pituitary gland], then you would be dwarfed in your size and would not live for a great time. In the beginning, prior to 455,000 years ago, this particular gland was mutated. In other words, it did not have the capacity then that it does now. There was no need to have it then. So in the beginning stages, if we were to see that which is termed a proper hologram of Homo erectus' brain, then we would be able to determine that that brain in those times did not have a seventh seal, that the seventh seal has become a graduated gland according to the use of energy.

So this is the brain. The yellow came when, as I told you, the Gods came and took you as primitive entities and commingled that which is termed their genes with yours. And the timeline from 455,000 to 40,000 years, that is what it took to get seeded into the human DNA that which is termed the differences of the DNA from your brothers and your sisters that gave you new physical possibilities. The first group of entities created from this cross-mutant were in the form of Mongolians. They were all olive-skinned and black-haired and some carried an enormous amount of body hair. It would not be until 40,000 years ago in your understanding, at the point in which Cro-Magnon's brain was utterly fixed, do we have now a diversity of that which is termed skin color, hair color, and eye color. This large neocortex is exactly what the Gods have. This is what they have. Some of them have a larger neocortex than Cro-Magnon, but this is what they gave you.

You have done little with this except used it automatically and genetically to operate your body, to operate your speech, to maintain balance, used it for memory. You have used it in its barest form. But the majority of the neocortex lies unmapped. It lies unmapped because it is waiting for something to happen. It is waiting for a realization to occur. And how does this transfer? This is not the day to go into a brain teaching. We will do that into your Retreat. But it is to say that the way that the brain is used today and the way you are going to use it this afternoon is that whatever sits right here in the frontal lobe, whatever sits there becomes reality because this place above the eyes and the brow, in science it is called the quiet area. That is the area that all those who are adept at meditation focus on. That is the area that they turn into. Whatever this brain puts here becomes law and as an Observer will affect all energy fields, keeping it status quo or changing it.

So now how does the brain do that? This yellow brain is created to fire holographic images. That is what thought is. And every neuron in your brain is hooked up to other neurons. Just to form the color yellow as a thought takes ten thousand and more neurons to fire simultaneously to give the color of a yellow sun. So now the brain is used to make images, make them, create them, imagine. The brain is an imagining machine. The neocortices make images. Those images that sit here are what precludes reality. It gives reality. It allows reality. It either eternalizes it or changes it. And this is what science calls the Observer.

When the scientist created the trick for the light and created an aperture in the opening of the veil, he did that while he was thinking about it.[14] That was his plan. He had a neuronet plan to follow. When he constructed the light to fall through, to be shown upon the veil, he knew there was a slit there. His brain fired the entire plan simultaneously. You call it thinking. But as a stream of thinking occurred, it was those thoughts about the plan that affected light and allowed light to move through the slit to the side of the negative screen. So whatever sits here [frontal lobe] is reality. So the yellow brain is a great architect. Its job is to design archetypes. Its job is to think coherently. Its job is to provide you, the Spirit, with as great amount of imagery as possible, because without it we don't collapse the wave into particle form. Got it?

Becoming Aware of Our Thought Processes

Now think about this for a moment. What if you were conscious every day of your thoughts? Most of you are unconscious of your thoughts. You are unconscious of the way you speak. You speak like barbarians, like trash, unbecoming to a God. You don't even use your words as force. But what if for a solid week you were observing the

_____
14 See Fig. 17: The Double-Slit Experiment.

way you thought? What if you got to do that? You would certainly see how a train of thought is the image that is necessary for creating life the way you have been experiencing it. So what if we change the picture? If we change the picture, we change reality. It is as simple as that. So the great runner I am going to send you this week is I am going to make you very conscious of your thinking for a week. So be it.

Now when I said to you last night, "Go and think of three things you would like," what did I tell you to do? I said, "Think." So you are sitting down and you are telling your brain, "Now pull up the files. What do we want, want, want, want? Let's see, what do we want, want? Oh, want, oh." Your brain is forming thoughts. At first you had something and then you tried to think of two more things. Did you know you are trying to think what you want? Isn't it interesting that you have to try to think of what you want? Why, if a genie appeared in front of you, you would be tongue-tied for the first five minutes. You can have anything you want. It is always safe to say, "If I can have anything I want, then everything I wish for after this I want, because that is the only thing I can think of this moment."

The brain is giving you images. When you decided what you want, you had to make your yellow brain be creative with you. And then it would give you an image, and you know what you did? You thought about the image. You know what else you did? You judged the image. "Oh, that will never happen. I don't deserve that. Oh, that is too much. Get real." That is what I am trying to tell you to do is to get real. So you put an image up and then you analyzed it. How many of you did that? How many of you analyzed what you wanted? Wouldn't you think that that is an ill-use of analysis now knowing what you know? What if you just created something and didn't judge it at all and said, "This is what I want." What would happen? What would happen? Would you get it? How many of you think you would? What would happen if you judged it? What if you were running an analysis on this hologram? What would happen? You don't get it. You know why? Because it is under analysis. It is under analysis. Even though it is sitting there, it is not permitted to do anything because it is being judged and weighed. It is being thought about, talked about. It is never left alone. As long as it is under analysis, it never manifests. How many of you understand that?

So think of the yellow brain as an archetype, a deliverer of images, and it puts it right here [frontal lobe]. Whatever goes here is in agreement with this entity here [Point Zero] always. It is from the back door in your brain that the energy comes, like through the kundalini, to give this total credibility. Without energy this doesn't go anywhere. If we allow it, we give it the greatest energy of all. If we discern it, we take away from it. We limit its energy.

Now here is what is very happy about this knowledge. When you truly understand how your brain works, how it affects energy and reality, what should become that which is termed apparent to you is that if it works for one thing it can work for everything. There is no law written anywhere that prohibits the use of that which is hidden in any area. You create everything. There is nothing impossible to you when you learn this science, when you learn the discipline. What, sadly, some people do is they never apply it. They are too lazy. But it works. If you can manifest a feather, you can manifest the ability to be Christ, as it is the same energy straight across the board.

I want you to eat like ravenous children. And attitude is everything. I want you to be happy with every chip you swallow, happy, happy. And when you have an opportunity, I want you to take a walk outside and clear your lungs, read, rest, and by the time that I come back have your three things narrowed down to a word each. I love you greatly.

Student: I love you.

Ramtha: I am worth it. That is all.

CHAPTER EIGHT
Closing Words

I greet the God within you. Pray let us never forget where it lives. Let's have a drink.

O my beloved God,
I do decree
that that which I focus upon
I surely want.
Manifest it straightaway.
So be it.
To life.

Be seated and let's go to work. The breath in the body spiritually represents the will of the Spirit. It is only when the Spirit is active in the body does the body have breath. When the Spirit pulls away from the body, the body no longer contains the breath of life. It is now understandable why in antiquity in order to connect with God, one always used the posture of stillness and the breath because the breath is the will of the Spirit. If we then can identify will, it is through that [the breath].

Now I want you to watch these three masters that I have up here on stage. I want you to watch them as they engage the breath in this posture.[1]

1 The description given in this book is for reference purposes only and it is not intended as a proper instruction and training in the discipline of C&E®. Students who wish to learn and practice Ramtha's discipline of C&E® must attend a class through Ramtha's School of Enlightenment and receive instruction personally.

FIG. 23: THE C&E® POSTURE

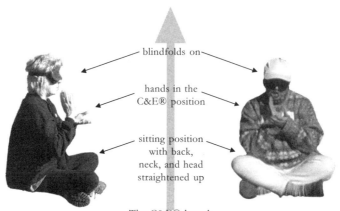

blindfolds on

hands in the
C&E® position

sitting position
with back,
neck, and head
straightened up

The C&E® breath
willfully forces energy up to the brain while
tightening down the lower abdomen and pressurizing
the air as it is released through the mouth.

Put your blindfolds on. Now make the triad.[2] We will
start with the triad.

Watch them very carefully. Look how they are sitting.
Watch everything they do.

Hold it. Now it doesn't seem too remarkable when you
are observing it, but what is going on with the entities? You
saw them breathe and breathe and breathe. Were they
thinking about you watching them? No. What were they
focused on? Moving that energy up. That is where their mind
was. Did you notice that two of them stopped breathing for
a moment? Did you wonder what they were doing? They
were assessing the feeling going through their body, whether

---

2 Beginning students are taught to make the sign of the triad with their blinders on
when they engage in any of the disciplines of the Great Work. The students begin
this discipline by pointing to their forehead, or seventh seal, which is the apex of
the triad. They continue to focus and complete the triad by moving their hand
slowly towards their left knee, then their right knee, and finally back to the forehead.
This triad represents the journey of involution and evolution.

the energy had gone into their head. We call that riding the light. They want to breathe so willfully and so purposefully that when they have stopped their focus and are just allowing, the energy moves into their head and their head grows very large. That is what they want to create.

When they have established this lighter-than-three-dimensional feeling, they are ready to do the work, but not until then. Did you notice their posture? Did you notice how they held their hands? Did you notice how they blew? Did you notice how still they were? If you do this correctly — It is possible for you to do this and do it with no focus at all, just become a habit. The only power you will get out of the habit in the beginning will be making the triad. But if you are not focused on empowering the breath, you will not feel a temperature change in your body, nor will you what we call ride the light, when you pause for a moment and let the energy rush into your head. All you will be doing is just blowing and blowing and thinking of something else. Then, like everything else, attitude is everything. In that case attitude was not in creating reality.

This discipline was done for you by three masters whose mind was into what they were doing, utterly and totally. They are not acting with you. They have retreated from you and have pulled in, and they are wanting to create reality.

The key to bringing about a powerful imaged focus is that the brain has to be prepared first. The body's frequency has to be elevated. When the body's frequency is elevated, the brain has moved to alpha frequency and we have will running in and out of the body. We can focus on anything and it will become so. So be it.

Now I want you to sit up straight, put your blindfolds on your forehead, sit up straight, and with this group you are going to practice the breath. We are going to put on a little music and all I want you to do is I want you, when you inhale, I want you to put your will behind your breath. I want you to open up your power so that your breath is all-powerful. And you work on that until I tell you to stop or I say, "Hold it." Practice with the music. Imitate what they have been doing because once you get it down, then I will show you how to manifest. When you are ready.

I will be most anxious when you can join us in a dance that is truly pagan, but that will come in your Retreat.

Now of all that I taught you that which is termed these two days — culminated into pouring forth that which is termed the substantialness of yourself, the God — all that I have told you will focus into a crystal truth when what you have created manifests. And if you are a charmed entity indeed, you are going to never forget this day nor what you have learned. And you will fall in love with magic, with God, and perhaps for the first time in your life you will wake up and realize what you have been missing. There is nothing that you cannot do. There is nothing impossible to you. If you have the mind, you have the brain to create it as an image, and you have the strength to hold it in spite of all outward reality, you will get it every time.

All of those great Gods that came along 455,000 years ago came this way. And they already knew this science way back then. They are evolved on the evolutionary scale. They are in a different kingdom, in a different life, possessing different bodies, with a great deal of longevity to their life. Some lived thousands of years without dying. That is your right. You are now coming to a place of understanding that they once came to. All that I have taught you works. If it were not so, all these people that belong to this school for so many years would not keep coming back.

And if God does live within you, then most certainly with this extraordinary amount of lengthy words that were brought forth these two days and all the writing and all the talking that you did, surely we have pinpointed the source of your divinity: Consciousness and energy create the nature of reality. The lists that you made today of what you wanted to change and what you wanted to have manifested for your life, I want you to put the date and your calendar year on those lists, and when you go home I want you to put them in a place that you see them every morning and every night. And as they manifest in your life, I want you to write down the day and the date that the manifestation came into fruition, because the only way you are ever going to believe in everything I have taught you is for you to experience it for yourself.

Now don't you get up tomorrow morning without first getting up a little early, going to a quiet place, putting your blindfolds on, and blowing like the wind, and create your day. Blow into your life power and strength and feel it. Then focus on something wonderful, perhaps that the day is an adventure and that by the end of the day you will have gained knowledge and will have grown. You practice what I have taught you, and if you like what you have learned, there is a great deal more to learn.[3] You hurry on back here to your Retreat. I will teach you wonderful things. Come with an open heart and a lot of room to grow. And in the meantime, remember me when the wind blows. Think of me when your runners come. And never, ever doubt that God lives within you ever again. Love I you greatly, masters. I am Ramtha the Enlightened One. This audience is over.

---

3 See the various books, audio recordings, and videos published by JZK Publishing, The Library of Ancient Wisdom, or contact Ramtha's School of Enlightenment for information about its courses and events.

Appendix — Workbook

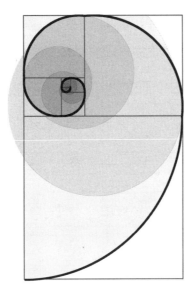

Instructions

It is important to color the following diagrams according to the color code provided for each drawing. This activity facilitates the ability to create clear, mental pictures of these fundamental concepts of Ramtha's teachings. The colored diagrams may be cut out and used for reference in the future or while reading this book.

Color Code

SEVEN LEVELS OF	CONSCIOUSNESS	& ENERGY	COLOR REFERENCE
7th Level	Ultraconsciousness	Infinite Unknown	Golden Rose
6th Level	Hyperconsciousness	Gamma Ray	Pale Rose
5th Level	Superconsciousness	X-Ray	Gold
4th Level	Bridge Consciousness	Ultraviolet Blue	Violet Blue
3rd Level	Conscious Awareness	Visible Light	Yellow
2nd Level	Social Consciousness	Infrared	Red
1st Level	Subconsciousness	Hertzian	Rusty Brown

Descent of Consciousness and Energy from Point Zero

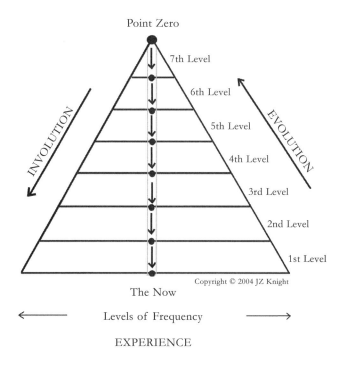

Point Zero

7th Level

6th Level

5th Level

4th Level

3rd Level

2nd Level

1st Level

INVOLUTION

EVOLUTION

The Now

⟵ ———— Levels of Frequency ———— ⟶

EXPERIENCE

Color Code

SEVEN LEVELS OF	CONSCIOUSNESS	& ENERGY	COLOR REFERENCE
7th Level	Ultraconsciousness	Infinite Unknown	Golden Rose
6th Level	Hyperconsciousness	Gamma Ray	Pale Rose
5th Level	Superconsciousness	X-Ray	Gold
4th Level	Bridge Consciousness	Ultraviolet Blue	Violet Blue
3rd Level	Conscious Awareness	Visible Light	Yellow
2nd Level	Social Consciousness	Infrared	Red
1st Level	Subconsciousness	Hertzian	Rusty Brown

Binary mind means two minds. It is the mind produced by accessing the knowledge of the human personality and the physical body without accessing our deep subconscious mind. Binary mind relies solely on the knowledge, perception, and thought processes of the neocortex and the first three seals. The fourth, fifth, sixth, and seventh seals remain closed in this state of mind.

Binary Mind — Living the Image

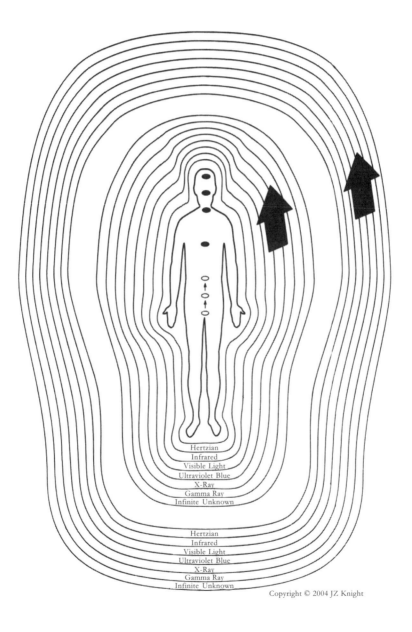

Hertzian
Infrared
Visible Light
Ultraviolet Blue
X-Ray
Gamma Ray
Infinite Unknown

Hertzian
Infrared
Visible Light
Ultraviolet Blue
X-Ray
Gamma Ray
Infinite Unknown

Color Code

SEVEN LEVELS OF	CONSCIOUSNESS	& ENERGY	COLOR REFERENCE
7th Level	Ultraconsciousness	Infinite Unknown	Golden Rose
6th Level	Hyperconsciousness	Gamma Ray	Pale Rose
5th Level	Superconsciousness	X-Ray	Gold
4th Level	Bridge Consciousness	Ultraviolet Blue	Violet Blue
3rd Level	Conscious Awareness	Visible Light	Yellow
2nd Level	Social Consciousness	Infrared	Red
1st Level	Subconsciousness	Hertzian	Rusty Brown

Analogical mind means one mind. It is the result of the alignment of primary consciousness and secondary consciousness, the Observer and the personality. The fourth, fifth, sixth, and seventh seals of the body are opened in this state of mind. The bands spin in opposite directions, like a wheel within a wheel, creating a powerful vortex that allows the thoughts held in the frontal lobe to coagulate and manifest.

Analogical Mind — Living in the Now

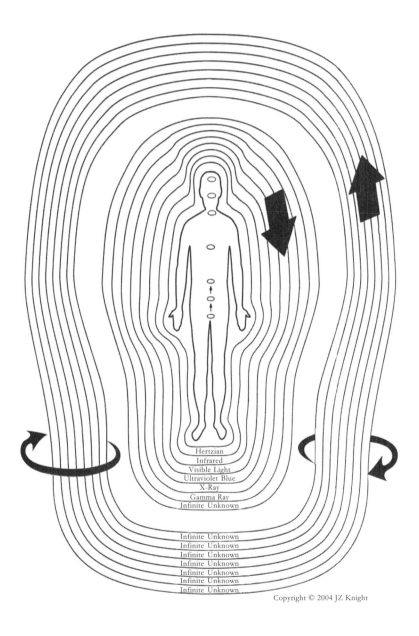

Hertzian
Infrared
Visible Light
Ultraviolet Blue
X-Ray
Gamma Ray
Infinite Unknown

Infinite Unknown
Infinite Unknown
Infinite Unknown
Infinite Unknown
Infinite Unknown
Infinite Unknown
Infinite Unknown

Color Code

BRAIN'S ANATOMY	COLOR REFERENCE
Neocortex	Yellow
Hypothalamus	Light Blue
Frontal Lobe	Yellow
Pituitary Gland	Royal Blue
Hippocampus and Amygdala	Indigo
Pons	Orange
Reticular Formation	Red
Midbrain	Orange
Thalamus	Blue
Corpus Callosum	Green
Pineal Gland	Purple
Lower Cerebellum	Red
Spinal Cord	Orange
Energy	Black

The Brain

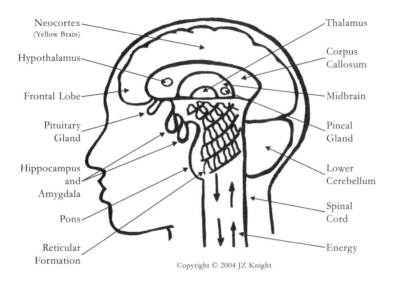

Neocortex
(Yellow Brain)

Hypothalamus

Frontal Lobe

Pituitary
Gland

Hippocampus
and
Amygdala

Pons

Reticular
Formation

Thalamus

Corpus
Callosum

Midbrain

Pineal
Gland

Lower
Cerebellum

Spinal
Cord

Energy

Copyright © 2004 JZ Knight

This is the original two-dimensional caricature-style drawing Ramtha used for his teaching on the function of the brain and its processes. He explained that the different aspects of the brain in this particular drawing are exaggerated and colorfully highlighted for the sake of study and understanding. This specific drawing became the standard tool used in all the subsequent teachings on the brain.

The Observer Effect and the Nerve Cell

The Observer is responsible
for collapsing the wave function of probability
into particle reality

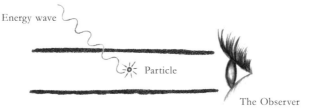

The act of observation
makes the nerve cells fire and produces thought

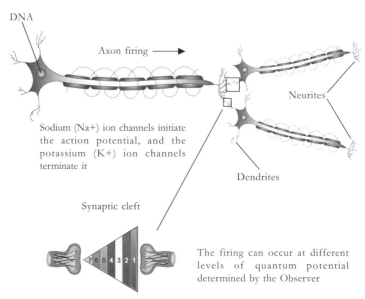

The Observer Effect and the Nerve Cell

(Reproduce here the notes and drawings from the previous page)

Cellular Biology and the Thought Connection

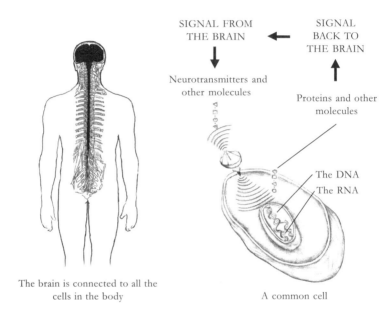

SIGNAL FROM THE BRAIN

SIGNAL BACK TO THE BRAIN

Neurotransmitters and other molecules

Proteins and other molecules

The DNA
The RNA

The brain is connected to all the cells in the body

A common cell

Cellular Biology and the Thought Connection

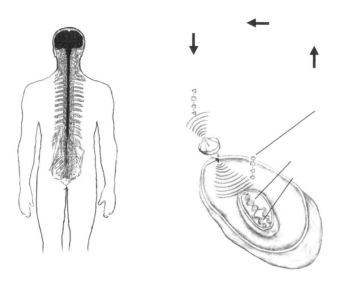

(Reproduce here the notes from the diagram on previous page)

Weblike Skeletal Structure of Cells

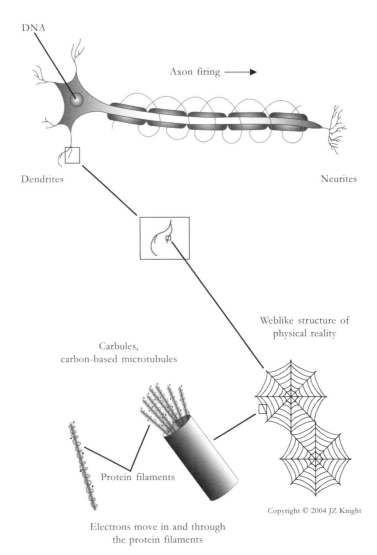

DNA

Axon firing ⟶

Dendrites

Neurites

Weblike structure of
physical reality

Carbules,
carbon-based microtubules

Protein filaments

Electrons move in and through
the protein filaments

Weblike Skeletal Structure of Cells

(Reproduce here the notes and drawings from the previous page)

The Blue Body®

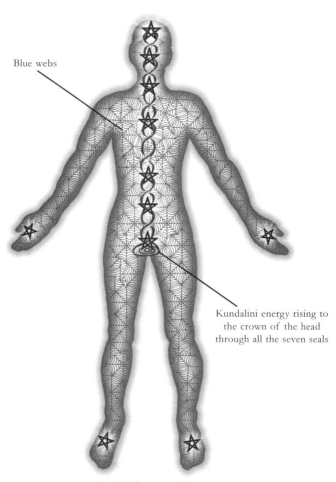

Blue webs

Kundalini energy rising to
the crown of the head
through all the seven seals

The Blue Body®

(Reproduce here the notes and drawings from the previous page)

RAMTHA'S GLOSSARY

Analogical. Being analogical means living in the Now. It is the creative moment and is outside of time, the past, and the emotions.

Analogical mind. Analogical mind means one mind. It is the result of the alignment of primary consciousness and secondary consciousness, the Observer and the personality. The fourth, fifth, sixth, and seventh seals of the body are opened in this state of mind. The bands spin in opposite directions, like a wheel within a wheel, creating a powerful vortex that allows the thoughts held in the frontal lobe to coagulate and manifest.

Bands, the. The bands are the two sets of seven frequencies that surround the human body and hold it together. Each of the seven frequency layers of each band corresponds to the seven seals of seven levels of consciousness in the human body. The bands are the auric field that allow the processes of binary and analogical mind.

Binary mind. This term means two minds. It is the mind produced by accessing the knowledge of the human personality and the physical body without accessing our deep subconscious mind. Binary mind relies solely on the knowledge, perception, and thought processes of the neocortex and the first three seals. The fourth, fifth, sixth, and seventh seals remain closed in this state of mind.

Blue Body®. It is the body that belongs to the fourth plane of existence, the bridge consciousness, and the ultraviolet frequency band. The Blue Body® is the lord over the lightbody and the physical plane.

Blue Body® Dance. It is a discipline taught by Ramtha in which the students lift their conscious awareness to the consciousness of the fourth plane. This discipline allows the Blue Body® to be accessed and the fourth seal to be opened.

Blue Body® Healing. It is a discipline taught by Ramtha in which the students lift their conscious awareness to the consciousness of the fourth plane and the Blue Body® for the purpose of healing or changing the physical body.

Blue webs. The blue webs represent the basic structure at a subtle level of the physical body. It is the invisible skeletal structure of the physical realm vibrating at the level of ultraviolet frequency.

Body/mind consciousness. Body/mind consciousness is the consciousness that belongs to the physical plane and the human body.

Book of Life. Ramtha refers to the soul as the Book of Life, where the whole journey of involution and evolution of each individual is recorded in the form of wisdom.

C&E® = R. Consciousness and energy create the nature of reality.

C&E®. Abbreviation of Consciousness & Energy^{SM}. This is the service mark of the fundamental discipline of manifestation and the raising of consciousness taught in Ramtha's School of Enlightenment. Through this discipline the students learn to create an analogical state of mind, open up their higher seals, and create reality from the Void. A Beginning C&E® Workshop is the name of the Introductory Workshop for beginning students in which they learn the fundamental concepts and disciplines of Ramtha's teachings. The teachings of the Beginning C&E® Workshop can be found in *Ramtha, A Beginner's Guide to Creating Reality,* third ed. (Yelm: JZK Publishing, a division of JZK, Inc., 2004), and in *Ramtha, Creating Personal Reality*, Tape 380 ed. (Yelm: Ramtha Dialogues, 1998).

Christwalk. The Christwalk is a discipline designed by Ramtha in which the student learns to walk very slowly being acutely aware. In this discipline the students learn to manifest, with each step they take, the mind of a Christ.

Consciousness. Consciousness is the child who was born from the Void's contemplation of itself. It is the essence and fabric of all being. Everything that exists originated in consciousness and manifested outwardly through its handmaiden energy. A stream of consciousness refers to the continuum of the mind of God.

Consciousness and energy. Consciousness and energy are the dynamic force of creation and are inextricably combined. Everything that exists originated in consciousness and manifested through the modulation of its energy impact into mass.

Create Your Day^{SM}. This is the service mark for a technique created by Ramtha for raising consciousness and energy and intentionally creating a constructive plan of experiences and events for the day early in the morning before the start of the day. This technique is exclusively taught at Ramtha's School of Enlightenment.

Disciplines of the Great Work. Ramtha's School of Ancient Wisdom is dedicated to the Great Work. The disciplines of the Great Work practiced in Ramtha's School of Enlightenment are all designed in their entirety by Ramtha. These practices are powerful initiations where the student has the opportunity to apply and experience firsthand the teachings of Ramtha.

Emotional body. The emotional body is the collection of past emotions, attitudes, and electrochemical patterns that make up the brain's neuronet and define the human personality of an individual. Ramtha describes it as the seduction of the unenlightened. It is the reason for cyclical reincarnation.

Emotions. An emotion is the physical, biochemical effect of an experience. Emotions belong to the past, for they are the expression of experiences that are already known and mapped in the neuropathways of the brain.

Energy. Energy is the counterpart of consciousness. All consciousness carries with it a dynamic energy impact, radiation, or natural expression of itself. Likewise, all forms of energy carry with it a consciousness that defines it.

Enlightenment. Enlightenment is the full realization of the human person, the attainment of immortality, and unlimited mind. It is the result of raising the kundalini energy sitting at the base of the spine to the seventh seal that opens the dormant parts of the brain. When the energy penetrates the lower cerebellum and the midbrain, and the subconscious mind is opened, the individual experiences a blinding flash of light called enlightenment.

Evolution. Evolution is the journey back home from the slowest levels of frequency and mass to the highest levels of consciousness and Point Zero.

Fieldwork®. Fieldwork® is one of the fundamental disciplines of Ramtha's School of Enlightenment. The students are taught to create a symbol of something they want to know and experience and draw it on a paper card. These cards are placed with the blank side facing out on the fence rails of a large field. The students blindfold themselves and focus on their symbol, allowing their body to walk freely to find their card through the application of the law of consciousness and energy and analogical mind.

Fifth plane. The fifth plane of existence is the plane of superconsciousness and x-ray frequency. It is also known as the Golden Plane or paradise.

Fifth seal. This seal is the center of our spiritual body that connects us to the fifth plane. It is associated with the thyroid gland and with speaking and living the truth without dualism.

First plane. It refers to the material or physical plane. It is the plane of the image consciousness and Hertzian frequency. It is the slowest and densest form of coagulated consciousness and energy.

First seal. The first seal is associated with the reproductive organs, sexuality, and survival.

First three seals. The first three seals are the seals of sexuality, pain and suffering, and controlling power. These are the seals commonly at play in all of the complexities of the human drama.

Fourth plane. The fourth plane of existence is the realm of the bridge consciousness and ultraviolet frequency. This plane is described as the plane of Shiva, the destroyer of the old and creator of the new. In this plane, energy is not yet split into positive and negative polarity. Any lasting changes or healing of the physical body must be changed first at the level of the fourth plane and the Blue Body®. This plane is also called the Blue Plane, or the plane of Shiva.

Fourth seal. The fourth seal is associated with unconditional love and the thymus gland. When this seal is activated, a hormone is released that maintains the body in perfect health and stops the aging process.

God. Ramtha's teachings are an exposition of the statement, "You are God." Humanity is described as the forgotten Gods, divine beings by nature who have forgotten their heritage and true identity. It is precisely this statement that represents Ramtha's challenging message to our modern age, an age riddled with religious superstition and misconceptions about the divine and the true knowledge of wisdom.

God within. It is the Observer, the great self, the primary consciousness, the Spirit, the God within the human person.

God/man. The full realization of a human being.

God/woman. The full realization of a human being.

Gods. The Gods are technologically advanced beings from other star systems who came to Earth 455,000 years ago. These Gods manipulated the human race genetically, mixing and modifying our DNA with theirs. They are responsible for the evolution of the neocortex and used the human race as a subdued work force. Evidence of these events is recorded in the Sumerian tablets and artifacts. This term is also used to describe the true identity of humanity, the forgotten Gods.

Golden body. It is the body that belongs to the fifth plane, superconsciousness, and x-ray frequency.

Great Work. The Great Work is the practical application of the knowledge of the Schools of Ancient Wisdom. It refers to the disciplines by which the human person becomes enlightened and is transmuted into an immortal, divine being.

Grid^SM, The. This is the service mark for a technique created by Ramtha for raising consciousness and energy and intentionally tapping into the Zero Point Energy field and the fabric of reality through a mental visualization. This technique is exclusively taught at Ramtha's School of Enlightenment.

Hierophant. A hierophant is a master teacher who is able to manifest what they teach and initiate their students into such knowledge.

Hyperconsciousness. Hyperconsciousness is the consciousness of the sixth plane and gamma ray frequency.

Infinite Unknown. It is the frequency band of the seventh plane of existence and ultraconsciousness.

Involution. Involution is the journey from Point Zero and the seventh plane to the slowest and densest levels of frequency and mass.

JZ Knight. JZ Knight is the only person appointed by Ramtha to channel him. Ramtha refers to JZ as his beloved daughter. She was Ramaya, the eldest of the children given to Ramtha during his lifetime.

Kundalini. Kundalini energy is the life force of a person that descends from the higher seals to the base of the spine at puberty. It is a large packet of energy reserved for human evolution, commonly pictured as a coiled serpent that sits at the base of the spine. This energy is different from the energy coming out of the first three seals responsible for sexuality, pain and suffering, power, and victimization. It is commonly described as the sleeping serpent or the sleeping dragon. The journey of the kundalini energy to the crown of the head is called the journey of enlightenment. This journey takes place when this serpent wakes up and starts to split and dance around the spine, ionizing the spinal fluid and changing its molecular structure. This action causes the opening of the midbrain and the door to the subconscious mind.

Life force. The life force is the Father/Mother, the Spirit, the breath of life within the person that is the platform from which the person creates its illusions, imagination, and dreams.

Life review. It is the review of the previous incarnation that occurs when the person reaches the third plane after death. The person gets the opportunity to be the Observer, the actor, and the recipient of its own actions. The unresolved issues from that lifetime that emerge at the life or light review set the agenda for the next incarnation.

Light, the. The light refers to the third plane of existence.

Lightbody. It is the same as the radiant body. It is the body that belongs to the third plane of conscious awareness and the visible light frequency band.

List, the. The List is the discipline taught by Ramtha where the student gets to write a list of items they desire to know and experience and then learn to focus on it in an analogical state of consciousness. The List is the map used to design, change, and reprogram the neuronet of the person. It is the tool that helps to bring meaningful and lasting changes in the person and their reality.

Make known the unknown. This phrase expresses the original divine mandate given to the Source consciousness to manifest and bring to conscious awareness all of the infinite potentials of the Void. This statement represents the basic intent that inspires the dynamic process of creation and evolution.

Mind. Mind is the product of streams of consciousness and energy acting on the brain creating thought-forms, holographic segments, or neurosynaptic patterns called memory. The streams of consciousness and energy are what keep the brain alive. They are its power source. A person's ability to think is what gives them a mind.

Mind of God. The mind of God comprises the mind and wisdom of every lifeform that ever lived on any dimension, in any time, or that ever will live on any planet, any star, or region of space.

Mirror consciousness. When Point Zero imitated the act of contemplation of the Void it created a mirror reflection of itself, a point of reference that made the exploration of the Void possible. It is called mirror consciousness or secondary consciousness. *See* **Self.**

Monkey-mind. Monkey-mind refers to the flickering, swinging mind of the personality.

Mother/Father Principle. It is the source of all life, the Father, the eternal Mother, the Void. In Ramtha's teachings, the Source and God the creator are not the same. God the creator is seen as Point Zero and primary consciousness but not as the Source, or the Void, itself.

Name-field. The name-field is the name of the large field where the discipline of Fieldwork® is practiced.

Neighborhood Walk^{SM}. This is the service mark of a technique created by JZ Knight for raising consciousness and energy and intentionally modifying our neuronets and set patterns of thinking no longer wanted and replacing them with new ones of our choice. This technique is exclusively taught at Ramtha's School of Enlightenment.

Neuronet. The contraction for "neural network," a network of neurons that perform a function together.

Observer. It refers to the Observer responsible for collapsing the particle/wave of quantum mechanics. It represents the great self, the Spirit, primary consciousness, the God within the human person.

Outrageous. Ramtha uses this word in a positive way to express something or someone who is extraordinary and unusual, unrestrained in action, and excessively bold or fierce.

People, places, things, times, and events. These are the main areas of human experience to which the personality is emotionally attached. These areas represent the past of the human person and constitute the content of the emotional body.

Personality, the. *See* **Emotional body.**

Plane of Bliss. It refers to the plane of rest where souls get to plan their next incarnations after their life reviews. It is also known as heaven and paradise where there is no suffering, no pain, no need or lack, and where every wish is immediately manifested.

Plane of demonstration. The physical plane is also called the plane of demonstration. It is the plane where the person has the opportunity to demonstrate its creative potentiality in mass and witness consciousness in material form in order to expand its emotional understanding.

Point Zero. It refers to the original point of awareness created by the Void through its act of contemplating itself. Point Zero is the original child of the Void, the birth of consciousness.

Primary consciousness. It is the Observer, the great self, the God within the human person.

Ram. Ram is a shorter version of the name Ramtha. Ramtha means the Father.

Ramaya. Ramtha refers to JZ Knight as his beloved daughter. She was Ramaya, the first one to become Ramtha's adopted child during his lifetime. Ramtha found Ramaya abandoned on the steppes of Russia. Many people gave their children to Ramtha during the march as a gesture of love and highest respect; these children were to be raised in the House of the Ram. His children grew to the great number of 133 even though he never had offspring of his own blood.

Ramtha (etymology). The name of Ramtha the Enlightened One, Lord of the Wind, means the Father. It also refers to the Ram who descended from the mountain on what is known as the terrible day of the Ram. "It is about that in all antiquity. And in ancient Egypt, there is an avenue dedicated to the Ram, the great conqueror. And they were wise enough to understand that whoever could walk down the avenue of the Ram could conquer the wind." The word Aram, the name of Noah's grandson, is formed from the Aramaic noun Araa — meaning earth, landmass — and the word Ramtha, meaning high. This Semitic name echoes Ramtha's descent from the high mountain, which began the great march.

Runner. A runner in Ramtha's lifetime was responsible for bringing specific messages or information. A master teacher has the ability to send runners to other people that manifest their words or intent in the form of an experience or an event.

Second plane. It is the plane of existence of social consciousness and the infrared frequency band. It is associated with pain and suffering. This plane is the negative polarity of the third plane of visible light frequency.

Second seal. This seal is the energy center of social consciousness and the infrared frequency band. It is associated with the experience of pain and suffering and is located in the lower abdominal area.

Secondary consciousness. When Point Zero imitated the act of contemplation of the Void it created a mirror reflection of itself, a point of reference that made the exploration of the Void possible. It is called mirror consciousness or secondary consciousness. *See* **Self.**

Self, the. The self is the true identity of the human person different from the personality. It is the transcendental aspect of the person. It refers to the secondary consciousness, the traveler in a journey of involution and evolution making known the unknown.

Sending-and-receiving. Sending-and-receiving is the name of the discipline taught by Ramtha in which the student learns to access information using the faculties of the midbrain to the exclusion of sensory perception. This discipline develops the student's psychic ability of telepathy and divination.

Seven seals. The seven seals are powerful energy centers that constitute seven levels of consciousness in the human body. The bands are the way in which the physical body is held together according to these seals. In every human being there is energy spiraling out of the first three seals or centers. The energy pulsating out of the first three seals manifests itself respectively as sexuality, pain, or power. When the upper seals are unlocked, a higher level of awareness is activated.

Seventh plane. The seventh plane is the plane of ultraconsciousness and the Infinite Unknown frequency band. This plane is where the journey of involution began. This plane was created by Point Zero when it imitated the act of contemplation of the Void and the mirror or secondary consciousness was created. A plane of existence or dimension of space and time exists between two points of consciousness. All the other planes were created by slowing down the time and frequency band of the seventh plane.

Seventh seal. This seal is associated with the crown of the head, the pituitary gland, and the attainment of enlightenment.

Shiva. The Lord God Shiva represents the Lord of the Blue Plane and the Blue Body®. Shiva is not used in reference to a singular deity from Hinduism. It is rather the representation of a state of consciousness that belongs to the fourth plane, the ultraviolet frequency band, and the opening of the fourth seal. Shiva is neither male nor female. It is an androgynous being, for the energy of the fourth plane has not yet been split into positive and negative polarity. This is an important distinction from the traditional Hindu representation of Shiva as a male deity who has a wife. The tiger skin at its feet, the trident staff, and the sun and the moon at the level of the head represent the mastery of this body over the first three seals of consciousness. The kundalini energy is pictured as fiery energy shooting from the base of the spine through the head. This is another distinction from some Hindu representations of Shiva with the serpent energy coming out at the level of the fifth seal or throat. Another symbolic image of Shiva is the long threads of dark hair and an abundance of pearl necklaces, which represent its richness of experience owned into wisdom. The quiver and bow and arrows are the agent by which Shiva shoots its powerful will and destroys imperfection and creates the new.

Sixth plane. The sixth plane is the realm of hyperconsciousness and the gamma ray frequency band. In this plane the awareness of being one with the whole of life is experienced.

Sixth seal. This seal is associated with the pineal gland and the gamma ray frequency band. The reticular formation that filters and veils the knowingness of the subconscious mind is opened when this seal is activated. The opening of the brain refers to the opening of this seal and the activation of its consciousness and energy.

Social consciousness. It is the consciousness of the second plane and the infrared frequency band. It is also called the image of the human personality and the mind of the first three seals. Social consciousness refers to the collective consciousness of human society. It is the collection of thoughts, assumptions, judgments, prejudices, laws, morality, values, attitudes, ideals, and emotions of the fraternity of the human race.

Soul. Ramtha refers to the soul as the Book of Life, where the whole journey of involution and evolution of the individual is recorded in the form of wisdom.

Subconscious mind. The seat of the subconscious mind is the lower cerebellum or reptilian brain. This part of the brain has its own independent connections to the frontal lobe and the whole of the body and has the power to access the mind of God, the wisdom of the ages.

Superconsciousness. This is the consciousness of the fifth plane and the x-ray frequency band.

Tahumo. Tahumo is the discipline taught by Ramtha in which the student learns the ability to master the effects of the natural environment — cold and heat — on the human body.

Tank field. It is the name of the large field with the labyrinth that is used for the discipline of The Tank®.

Tank®, The. It is the name given to the labyrinth used as part of the disciplines of Ramtha's School of Enlightenment. The students are taught to find the entry to this labyrinth blindfolded and move through it focusing on the Void without touching the walls or using the eyes or the senses. The objective of this discipline is to find, blindfolded, the center of the labyrinth or a room designated and representative of the Void.

Third plane. This is the plane of conscious awareness and the visible light frequency band. It is also known as the light plane and the mental plane. When the energy of the Blue Plane is lowered down to this frequency band, it splits into positive and negative polarity. It is at this point that the soul splits into two, giving origin to the phenomenon of soulmates.

Third seal. This seal is the energy center of conscious awareness and the visible light frequency band. It is associated with control, tyranny, victimization, and power. It is located in the region of the solar plexus.

Thought. Thought is different from consciousness. The brain processes a stream of consciousness, modifying it into segments — holographic pictures — of neurological, electrical, and chemical prints called thoughts. Thoughts are the building blocks of mind.

Torsion Process[SM]. This is the service mark of a technique created by Ramtha for raising consciousness and energy and intentionally creating a torsion field using the mind. Through this technique the student learns to build a wormhole in space/time, alter reality, and create dimensional phenomena such as invisibility, levitation, bilocation, teleportation, and others. This technique is exclusively taught at Ramtha's School of Enlightenment.

Twilight®. This term is used to describe the discipline taught by Ramtha in which the students learn to put their bodies in a catatonic state similar to deep sleep, yet retaining their conscious awareness.

Twilight® Visualization Process. It is the process used to practice the discipline of the List or other visualization formats.

Ultraconsciousness. It is the consciousness of the seventh plane and the Infinite Unknown frequency band. It is the consciousness of an ascended master.

Unknown God. The Unknown God was the single God of Ramtha's ancestors, the Lemurians. The Unknown God also represents the forgotten divinity and divine origin of the human person.

Upper four seals. The upper four seals are the fourth, fifth, sixth, and seventh seals.

Void, the. The Void is defined as one vast nothing materially, yet all things potentially. *See* **Mother/Father Principle.**

Yellow brain. The yellow brain is Ramtha's name for the neocortex, the house of analytical and emotional thought. The reason why it is called the yellow brain is because the neocortices were colored yellow in the original two-dimensional, caricature-style drawing Ramtha used for his teaching on the function of the brain and its processes. He explained that the different aspects of the brain in this particular drawing are exaggerated and colorfully highlighted for the sake of study and understanding. This specific drawing became the standard tool used in all the subsequent teachings on the brain.

Yeshua ben Joseph. Ramtha refers to Jesus Christ by the name Yeshua ben Joseph, following the Jewish traditions of that time.

BIBLIOGRAPHY

Alford, Alan F. *Gods of the New Millennium, Scientific Proof of Flesh &* *Blood Gods*. England: Eridu Books, 1996.

Bohm, David. *Wholeness and the Implicate Order*. London: Routledge, 1980.

Davies, Stevan L. *The Gospel of Thomas and Christian Wisdom*. New York: Seabury Press, 1983.

De la Cruz, Juan. *Obras Completas*. 4th ed. Madrid: Editorial de Spiritualidad, 1992.

De la Cruz, Juan. *The Collected Works*. Washington, D.C.: Institute of Carmelite Studies, 1979.

De León, Luis. *De los Nombres de Cristo*. Edited by Antonio Sánchez Zamarreño. Madrid: Espasa Calpe, 1991.

Goswami, Amit. *The Self-Aware Universe*. New York: Tarcher/ Putnam, 1995.

Grof, Christina and Stanislav. *The Adventure of Self Discovery*. New York: State University of New York Press, 1988.

———. *The Stormy Search for the Self*. London: HarperCollins, 1991.

Guillaumont, A. *et al*. *The Gospel According to Thomas, Coptic Text Established and Translated*. London: Collins, 1959

Henry, Martin. *On Not Understanding God*. Dublin: Columba Press, 1997.

Hirschberger, Johannes. *Historia de la Filosofía*. Vol. 1, *Antigüedad, Edad Media, Renacimiento*. Barcelona: Editorial Herder, 1994.

In Search of the Self: The Role of Consciousness in the Construction of Reality, a Conference on Contemporary Spirituality. February 8-9, 1997, Yelm, Washington. Video ed. Yelm: JZK Publishing, a division of JZK, Inc., 1997.

JZ Knight and Ramtha: Intimate Conversations. Video ed. Yelm: JZK Publishing, a division of JZK, Inc., 1998.

Kasper, Walter. *Jesus the Christ*. London: Burns & Oates, 1976.

Knight, JZ. *A State of Mind — My Story*. Yelm: JZK Publishing, a division of JZK, Inc., 2004.

Krippner, Stanley, Ian Wickramasekera, Judy Wickramasekera, and Charles W. Winstead, III. "The Ramtha Phenomenon: Psychological, Phenomenological, and Geomagnetic Data." In *The Journal of the American Society for Psychical Research*, Vol. 92, No. 1, January 1998.

Layton, Bentley. *The Gnostic Scriptures*. The Anchor Bible Reference Library ed. New York: Doubleday, 1987.

Melton, J. Gordon. *Finding Enlightenment, Ramtha's School of Ancient Wisdom*. Hillsboro: Beyond Words Publishing, 1998.

New Jerusalem Bible.

Platón. *Dialogos*. 22nd ed. Edited by Colección Austral. México: Espasa Calpe, 1984.

Ramtha, A Beginner's Guide to Creating Reality. Revised and expanded ed. Yelm: JZK Publishing, a division of JZK, Inc., 2000.

Ramtha, A Master's Reflection on the History of Humanity. Part I, *Human Civilization, Origins and Evolution*. Yelm: JZK Publishing, a division of JZK, Inc., 2001.

Ramtha, A Master's Reflection on the History of Humanity. Part II, *Rediscovering the Pearl of Ancient Wisdom*. Yelm: JZK Publishing, a division of JZK, Inc., 2002.

Ramtha, Beginning C&E® Workshop. Tape 324 ed. Yelm: Ramtha Dialogues, 1995.

Ramtha, Beginning C&E® Workshop. Tape 326 ed. Yelm: Ramtha Dialogues, 1996.

Ramtha, Blue College Retreat. Tape 443.4 restricted ed. Yelm: Ramtha Dialogues, 2000.

Ramtha, Blue College Weekend. Tape 437 restricted ed. Yelm: Ramtha Dialogues, 2000.

Ramtha, Creating Personal Reality. Tape 380 ed. Yelm: Ramtha Dialogues, 1998.

Ramtha, Creation. Specialty Tape 005 ed. Yelm: Ramtha Dialogues, 1980.

Ramtha, Our Omnipotent Spirit: Direct Line to the Power of Manifestation. Tape 327.09 ed. Yelm: Ramtha Dialogues, 1996.

Ramtha, Preserving Oneself. Tape 304 ed. Yelm: Ramtha Dialogues, 1991.

Ramtha, That Elixir Called Love. Yelm: JZK Publishing, a division of JZK, Inc., 2003.

Ramtha, The Mystery of Birth and Death, Redefining the Self. Yelm: JZK Publishing, a division of JZK, Inc., 2000.

Ramtha, The Observer Part I. Tape 376 ed. Yelm: Ramtha Dialogues, 1998.

Ramtha, The White Book. Yelm: JZK Publishing, a division of JZK, Inc., 2004.

Ramtha, Walking the Journey of the Woman. Tape 437.1 ed. Yelm: Ramtha Dialogues, 2000.

Ramtha's Introduction to the World Tour. Video ed. Yelm: JZK Publishing, a division of JZK, Inc., 1998.

Ramtha's Lifetime. Specialty Tape 021 ed. Yelm: Ramtha Dialogues, 1984.

Reese, William L. *Dictionary of Philosophy and Religion, Eastern and Western Thought.* Expanded ed. New York: Humanity Books, 1999.

Santos Otero, Aurelio de. *Los Evangelios Apócrifos: Colección de Textos Griegos y Latinos, Versión Crítica, Estudios Introductorios y Comentarios.* 9th ed. Madrid: Biblioteca de Autores Cristianos, 1996.

Schrödter, Willy. *A Rosicrucian Notebook.* York Beach: Samuel Weiser, Inc., 1991.

Talbot, Michael. *The Holographic Universe.* New York: HarperCollins, 1992.

The Portable Jung. Edited by Joseph Campbell. New York: Penguin Books, 1976.

The Works of Plato. Edited by Irwin Edman. New York: Modern Library, 1956.

The World of Michelangelo, 1475-1564. Edited by Robert Coughlan. New York: Time-Life Books, Inc., 1966.

Tillich, Paul. *Systematic Theology, Combined Volume.* London: James Nisbet and Company Limited, 1968.

Tolkien, J.R.R. *The Lord of the Rings.* London: Grafton, 1991.

Waite, Arthur Edward. *Real History of the Rosicrucians.* New York: Steinerbooks, 1982.

Wolf, Fred Alan. *Parallel Universes.* New York: Simon & Schuster, 1990.

———. *Taking the Quantum Leap.* New York: Perennial Library, 1989.

———. *The Spiritual Universe.* Portsmouth: Moment Point Press, Inc.,1999.

Zukav, Gary. *The Dancing Wu Li Masters.* New York: Bantam Books, 1980.

LIST OF SOURCES

The main concern in preparing Ramtha's teachings for publication in printed form has been to render them as much as possible in the context and form in which they were delivered. Great care has been taken to avoid altering and changing the meaning of the teachings by taking them out of their context or by even introducing a system of punctuation that would change the meaning.

The contents of this book are based on Ramtha Dialogues®, a series of magnetic recordings of Ramtha in session with his students, registered with the United States Copyright Office, with permission from JZ Knight and JZK, Inc. The excerpts from the various events that were used in the chapters of this book were left in their original dialogue format as they took place when they were delivered by Ramtha, except for Chapter 1 in *Part I: Ramtha, a Master's Journey to Enlightenment*. Chapter 1 was taken from *Ramtha's Lifetime*, Specialty Tape 021 ed. Yelm: Ramtha Dialogues, 1984. This tape is a collection of questions and answers relating to Ramtha's own lifetime. Some of these questions often cover the same events in Ramtha's life. The material was edited and arranged in chronological order to make the story flow. Nevertheless, it is important to note that any editing done by JZK Publishing, a division of JZK, Inc., never includes additions to the original words delivered by Ramtha. All the chapters in *Part II: Fundamental Concepts of Ramtha's Teachings,* were taken from *Beginning C&E®*

Workshop, February 3-4, 1996, Tape 326 ed. Yelm: Ramtha Dialogues, 1996. Ramtha uses the aid of drawings and pictures to teach and explain abstract concepts like the Void, consciousness, time, energy, space, et cetera. We have included the pictures and drawings that were used at this particular event throughout the book. We have also provided the most fundamental ones in the Workbook in the Appendix to facilitate their reference. Ramtha, in the course of his dissertation, points to a particular place in a drawing, using the words "here," "this," "these," or "that." We have incorporated these references to the text in brackets and in footnotes. The publisher's objective is to provide the readers with the opportunity to participate in and experience the session as if they had been present.

Ramtha often redefines the language he uses to teach by coining new words. The meaning of these coined words becomes clear within the context of his teaching, and the particular teaching becomes clarified also by the use of such uncommon words. We have constructed a Glossary of terms and concepts which Ramtha uses in a qualified way to facilitate the correct interpretation of his teachings. We have also provided a detailed Index to allow the reader to reference specific topics of interest covered in this book and to encourage the research study of this material. This book is intended to serve as the general introduction to Ramtha and his School of Ancient Wisdom dedicated to the Great Work.

INDEX

A

abstinence 200

Adam and Eve 191

addiction 201, 208, 212

advertising 26

Akhnaton, Pharaoh 51

Albigenses 51

alpha state. *See* brain

alphabet 23

altered ego 74, 101, 112, 137-138, 148

altered states of awareness 33

America 63-64, 209

American Indians 66, 69

American Psychological Association 34

amnesia 48, 202

amygdala. *See* brain's anatomy

analogical mind 22, 112

anarchy 207

anatomy

heart 30, 33

spinal column 149, 242, 244-245, 247-248, 251

spinal fluid 243-244

ancient wisdom 23, 242, 244, 265, 268

angel 178

anger. *See* emotions

anxiety/worry. *See* emotions

Apollonius of Tyana 51

Aramaic 41

archetype 258, 260

aristocracy 73

Aristotle (philosopher) 47

arrogance. *See* attitude

art 35, 51, 180, 183

ascension 28, 61, 84-85, 114-115, 132, 234

Ascent of Mount Carmel, The 51

Association for Applied Psychophysiology and Biofeedback 33

astronomy 156, 163, 170, 179-180

Atlantis 61-69, 73

Atlatians 63-66, 68, 70, 77, 79, 118

atom 191-192, 196, 220-221, 228, 233-234, 246, 248, 252, 255

electron 191-192, 220, 228, 233, 255

forgiveness 95-96, 119-120, 136, 199-200
fourth plane. *See* planes of existence
Francis of Assisi 51
free space 234
freedom 28, 43, 96, 109-110, 113-114, 194, 196, 199-200, 210, 247
frequency 48, 71, 73, 111, 116, 143, 162-166, 168, 170, 173, 178, 217-218, 220, 231, 233-234, 267
  hertz 166, 178, 252
  Infinite Unknown 234
  infrared 179, 232, 252
  visible light spectrum 143, 192, 198, 232, 234, 253-254
Freud, Sigmund 24
frontal lobe. *See* brain's anatomy

G

galaxy 138, 154, 190
Genesis, the book of. *See* Bible, the
genetic manipulation 180-181, 257
genetics 71, 74, 118, 132, 175, 180-183, 194-195, 256-257
genius 30
German idealism 38
glands 111, 253, 256
Gnosticism 22, 36, 48
God 15-17, 24, 27-28, 30-32, 38, 41-42, 45, 47-48, 51-52, 54, 72, 75, 77, 99, 101, 106, 112, 116, 119-121, 128, 130-134, 136, 142-143, 149, 154, 158, 162-163, 166, 172, 176-178, 182-184, 198-199, 205-206, 208-210, 234-235, 246, 265, 268
  God/man, God/woman realized 30-31, 56, 114, 132, 209, 222, 229, 234
  the forgotten Gods 16, 25, 50, 154, 202, 209, 225
  word of God 41
God within you 16-17, 21, 25, 27, 37, 44, 48, 55, 87, 96, 117, 127, 131, 133, 136-137, 146, 153, 175, 183-184, 197, 200, 202, 205-206, 229, 234, 265, 268-269
Gods and Goddesses 16, 72, 91, 115-116, 130, 179-183, 256, 268
golden body. *See* planes of existence
good and evil 21, 48, 176, 178, 189
Gospel according to John. *See* Bible, the
Great Work, the 15-16, 21, 49, 150, 201, 210, 267
Greece 22
Greek 23, 43
guilt. *See* emotions
Gustavian Monoculus 95

H

habit 267
hallucinogenics 254
Harley, Gail 34

N

Ramtha's School of Enlightenment
The Original School of Consciousness & Energy^{SM}

For more information:
Toll Free: (800) 347.0439
Tel: (360) 458.5201 ext. 10
Fax: (360) 458.2183
14507 Yelm Hwy. SE
P.O. Box 1210
Yelm, Washington 98597
Email: registration@ramtha.com
www.ramtha.com

JZK Publishing
A Division of JZK, Inc.

P.O. Box 1210
Yelm, Washington 98597
360.458.5201
800.347.0439
www.ramtha.com
www.jzkpublishing.com